PIONEERS IN MATHEMATICS

THE FOUNDATIONS
OF MATHEMATICS

1800 to 1900

MICHAEL J. BRADLEY, PH.D.

CHELSEA HOUSE
PUBLISHERS
An imprint of Infobase Publishing

The Foundations of Mathematics: 1800 to 1900

Chelsea House
An imprint of Infobase Publishing
132 West 31st Street
New York NY 10001

Library of Congress Cataloging-in-Publication Data

Bradley, Michael J. (Michael John), 1956-
    The foundations of mathematics: 1800 to 1900 / Michael J. Bradley.
        p. cm.—(Pioneers in mathematics)
    Includes bibliographical references and index.
    ISBN 0-8160-5425-8 (acid-free paper)
    1. Mathematicians—Biography. 2. Mathematics—History—19th century.
3. Mathematical analysis—Foundations. I. Title. II. Series: Bradley, Michael J.
(Michael John), 1956-   . Pioneers in mathematics.
    QA28.B735 2006
    [B]510.92'2—dc22   2005033736

Text design by Mary Susan Ryan-Flynn
Cover design by Dorothy Preston
Illustrations by Dale Williams

Printed in the United States of America

MP FOF 10 9 8 7 6 5 4 3 2 1

This book is printed on acid-free paper.

CONTENTS

PREFACE

Mathematics is a human endeavor. Behind its numbers, equations, formulas, and theorems are the stories of the people who expanded the frontiers of humanity's mathematical knowledge. Some were child prodigies while others developed their aptitudes for mathematics later in life. They were rich and poor, male and female, well educated and self-taught. They worked as professors, clerks, farmers, engineers, astronomers, nurses, and philosophers. The diversity of their backgrounds testifies that mathematical talent is independent of nationality, ethnicity, religion, class, gender, or disability.

Pioneers in Mathematics is a five-volume set that profiles the lives of 50 individuals, each of whom played a role in the development and the advancement of mathematics. The overall profiles do not represent the 50 most notable mathematicians; rather, they are a collection of individuals whose life stories and significant contributions to mathematics will interest and inform middle school and high school students. Collectively, they represent the diverse talents of the millions of people, both anonymous and well known, who developed new techniques, discovered innovative ideas, and extended known mathematical theories while facing challenges and overcoming obstacles.

Each book in the set presents the lives and accomplishments of 10 mathematicians who lived during an historical period. *The Birth of Mathematics* profiles individuals from ancient Greece, India, Arabia, and medieval Italy who lived from 700 B.C.E. to 1300 C.E. *The Age of Genius* features mathematicians from Iran, France, England, Germany, Switzerland, and America who lived between the 14th and 18th centuries. *The Foundations of Mathematics* presents

19th-century mathematicians from various European countries. *Modern Mathematics* and *Mathematics Frontiers* profile a variety of international mathematicians who worked in the early 20th and the late 20th century, respectively.

The 50 chapters of Pioneers in Mathematics tell pieces of the story of humankind's attempt to understand the world in terms of numbers, patterns, and equations. Some of the individuals profiled contributed innovative ideas that gave birth to new branches of mathematics. Others solved problems that had puzzled mathematicians for centuries. Some wrote books that influenced the teaching of mathematics for hundreds of years. Still others were among the first of their race, gender, or nationality to achieve recognition for their mathematical accomplishments. Each one was an innovator who broke new ground and enabled their successors to progress even further.

From the introduction of the base-10 number system to the development of logarithms, calculus, and computers, most significant ideas in mathematics developed gradually, with countless individuals making important contributions. Many mathematical ideas developed independently in different civilizations separated by geography and time. Within the same civilization, the name of the scholar who developed a particular innovation often became lost as his idea was incorporated into the writings of a later mathematician. For these reasons, it is not always possible to identify accurately any one individual as the first person to have discovered a particular theorem or to have introduced a certain idea. But then mathematics was not created by one person or for one person; it is a human endeavor.

ACKNOWLEDGMENTS

An author does not write in isolation. I owe a debt of thanks to so many people who helped in a myriad of ways during the creation of this work.

To Jim Tanton, who introduced me to this fascinating project.

To Jodie Rhodes, my agent, who put me in touch with Facts On File and handled the contractual paperwork.

To Frank K. Darmstadt, my editor, who kept me on track throughout the course of this project.

To Candace Austin, who thoroughly researched the material for the chapter on Marie-Sophie Germain.

To M. V. Moorthy, who thoroughly researched the material for the chapter on Georg Cantor.

To Dan Gries, who created the torus illustrations for the chapter on Henri Poincaré.

To Larry Gillooly, George Heffernan, Sylvie Pressman, Suzanne Scholz, Ernie Montella, and Warren Kay, who assisted with the translations of Latin, Italian, French, and German titles.

To Steve Scherwatzky, who helped me to become a better writer by critiquing early drafts of many chapters.

To Melissa Cullen-DuPont, who provided valuable assistance with the artwork.

To my wife, Arleen, who provided constant love and support.

To many relatives, colleagues, students, and friends who inquired and really cared about my progress on this project.

To Joyce Sullivan, Donna Katzman, and their students at Sacred Heart School in Lawrence, Massachusetts who created poster presentations for a Math Fair based on some of these chapters.

To John Tabak, Kit Moser, Tucker McElroy, and Tobi Zausher, who shared helpful suggestions for locating sources of photographs and illustrations.

To the faculty and administration of Merrimack College, who created the Faculty Sabbatical Program and the Faculty Development Grant Program, both of which provided me with time to read and write.

INTRODUCTION

The Foundations of Mathematics, the third volume of the Pioneers in Mathematics set, profiles the lives of 10 mathematicians who lived between 1800 and 1900 C.E. Each one contributed to one or more of the four major initiatives that characterized the rapid growth of mathematics during the 19th century: the introduction of rigor, the investigation of the structure of mathematical systems, the development of new branches of mathematics, and the spread of mathematical activity throughout Europe.

During the previous two centuries mathematicians had developed a wealth of new ideas but had not carefully employed rigorous definitions, proofs, and procedures. In the early 19th century mathematicians recognized the need to precisely define their terms, to logically prove even the most obvious principles, and to use rigorous methods of manipulation. They restored to mathematics the meticulous logic and precision that had characterized classic geometry 2,000 years earlier. German mathematician Carl Friedrich Gauss's proofs of the fundamental theorem of arithmetic and the fundamental theorem of algebra formally established elementary principles in these two branches of mathematics. Norwegian mathematician Niels Abel developed rigorous methods for determining the convergence of infinite series, one of the basic principles of calculus. German mathematician Georg Cantor provided a definition for the fundamental concept of a real number and proved the existence of different degrees of infinity.

The insistence on careful attention to details led 19th-century mathematicians to reconsider the structure of mathematical systems. Gauss and several other mathematicians recognized that the parallel postulate was independent of the other axioms of Euclidean geometry and that alternative systems of non-Euclidean geometry existed. Abel and French mathematician Évariste Galois discovered that the solutions of polynomial equations were related to groups of permutations and that the structure of those groups corresponded to properties of the equations. Cantor's work with the axioms of set theory led to a reconsideration of the structure of all of mathematics.

In concert with their investigations of the structure of mathematical systems, 19th-century mathematicians developed new branches of the discipline. Galois's ideas led to the development of group theory. Abel's work established functional analysis. Cantor's innovations marked the founding of set theory. French mathematician Henri Poincaré introduced a range of new ideas that established algebraic topology, chaos theory, and the theory of several complex variables as new branches of mathematics. English nurse Florence Nightingale demonstrated that the new branch of mathematics known as statistics could be used effectively as a basis for making positive changes in societal practices. English mathematician Ada Lovelace produced the first explanation of the process of computer programming.

The fourth aspect of mathematics that was evident during the 19th century was the spread of mathematical activity throughout Europe. No longer an elite domain reserved for highly trained scholars at a small number of academic institutions and occasional amateur mathematicians, mathematics became accessible to all educated people. Although France and Germany remained the leading countries for the training of mathematicians and the development of new mathematical ideas, nearly every European country established universities, national academies, and scholarly institutes. The growing number of mathematical journals, professional societies, and international conferences provided opportunities for the wide exchange of mathematical ideas. A small but growing number of women started to make contributions to the advancement of the discipline. Russian mathematician Sonya Kovalevsky proved a fundamental theorem in differential equations. French mathematician Marie-Sophie Germain investigated prime numbers and the theory of vibrating surfaces. Scottish mathematician Mary Somerville wrote four books on astronomy, the physical sciences, geography, and microscopic structures, which made advanced scientific theories accessible to the general public.

During the 19th century mathematics in Europe matured into a rigorous discipline that attracted widespread participation in almost all countries on the Continent. Formalizing the foundational structure of mathematics enabled the introduction of new branches of the discipline. The 10 individuals profiled in this volume represent the thousands of scholars who made modest and momentous mathematical discoveries that advanced the world's knowledge. The stories of their achievements provide a glimpse into the lives and the minds of some of the pioneers who discovered mathematics.

Marie-Sophie Germain

(1776–1831)

Marie-Sophie Germain solved Fermat's Last Theorem for a class of prime numbers that were named after her and won a prize for her research on the mathematical theory of vibrating surfaces.
(The Granger Collection)

Discoveries in Prime Numbers and Elasticity

Although she was a reclusive, self-taught mathematician, Sophie Germain earned the respect and friendship of Europe's leading mathematicians. She identified a class of prime numbers that bear her name. Through Germain's Theorem she made a significant contribution toward the proof of Fermat's Last Theorem. Her paper on the mathematical theory of vibrating surfaces won the grand prize in France's national competition. She introduced the concept of mean curvature of a surface.

Early Education

Marie-Sophie Germain was born on April 1, 1776, in Paris, France. Ambroise-François Germain, her father, was involved in national politics, serving as a representative in the States-General and in the Constituent Assembly during the French Revolution. He was also a prosperous businessman and became the director of the Bank of France. Marie-Madeleine Gruguelu Germain, her mother, raised Sophie and her two sisters, Marie-Madeleine and Angelique-Ambroise. The Germain's large house had a library filled with books on many subjects and private bedrooms for each of the three girls.

The era in which Sophie grew up was a time of revolution and change. During her childhood, French armies helped Americans fight for their independence from England. Throughout her teen-age years, from 1789 to 1799, the French Revolution violently changed the lives of the people of France. During the Reign of Terror, from September 1793 to July 1794, the Committee on Public Safety arrested 200,000 citizens and executed between 20,000 and 40,000 of them at the guillotine. To escape this turmoil, Sophie spent most of her time reading in her family's library.

When she was 13 years old, she read about Archimedes, the Greek mathematician and scientist who made many discoveries in geometry and physics. According to the story, while the Roman army was invading the Greek city of Syracuse, Archimedes was drawing mathematical diagrams in the sand. He was so absorbed in solving the problem that when a soldier ordered him to get up and come with him, Archimedes insisted that the soldier move out of his light and let him finish the problem. The angry soldier killed Archimedes with his spear.

The story of Archimedes' death made a deep impact on Sophie. She wondered what could be so fascinating about mathematics that a person would risk losing his life. Inspired by Archimedes, Sophie became determined to study mathematics despite her parents' prohibitions. Like most European parents in the 18th century, they believed it was not an appropriate subject for a young woman to study and they feared that it might damage her mind. When they discovered that she was taking math books to her room and studying at night, they stopped lighting the fire in her room's fireplace, took away her clothes after she went to bed, and removed the oil lamps from her room. Despite these restrictions, Sophie wrapped herself in blankets, lit candles that she had hidden in her room, and read math books that she had secretly borrowed from the library. One morning, her parents found her asleep at her desk, her room so cold that the ink had frozen in the inkwell. They agreed to allow their determined daughter to pursue her passion for mathematics.

With her new freedom to study, Sophie read every mathematics book in her family's library. Studying books such as Étienne Bézout's *Traité d'Arithmétique* (Treatise on arithmetic) she learned geometry and algebra. She taught herself Latin so she could read the classic works of Sir Isaac Newton and Leonhard Euler. Eventually her parents became very supportive of her mathematical studies. When she read Jacques Antoine-Joseph Cousin's *Le Calcul Différential* (Differential calculus), they arranged for the author to visit her, providing her much-needed encouragement.

Monsieur Le Blanc

In 1794 mathematicians Lazare Carnot and Gaspard Monge established a new school in Paris called École Polytechnique (Polytechnic University) to provide the highest quality training in mathematics and science for the country's most talented young men. Although Germain was not permitted to attend classes at this institution, she became friends with some students who shared their lecture notes and their homework with her. Germain submitted her homework solutions signed with the name Antoine-August Le Blanc, a student who had dropped out of school. When Professor Joseph-Louis Lagrange corrected her final project at the end of his mathematical analysis course, he was impressed with the excellent work that had been submitted by "Monsieur Le Blanc." ("Monsieur" means "Mister" in French.) After the students told him that Monsieur Le Blanc was actually a young woman who had been studying on her own, he insisted that he had to meet her.

Lagrange visited Germain at her family's home, encouraged her to continue her mathematical studies, and agreed to be her mentor, assisting her in any way that he could. Although he was not able to permit her to take his courses, he recommended books and research papers for her to read, met with her to explain difficult concepts, and wrote frequent letters to her. Most important, he introduced her to many of Europe's leading mathematicians.

As Germain studied Adrien-Marie Legendre's 1798 book *Essai sur le théorie des nombres* (Essay on the theory of numbers), she developed some additional ideas and techniques. Lagrange arranged for her to write to Legendre, who was impressed with her discoveries. Through a series of letters, he helped her to more fully develop the concepts she had formulated. Their correspondence eventually became a collaboration of mathematical partners.

German mathematician Carl Friedrich Gauss also encouraged and advised Germain through a series of letters that he wrote to her between 1804 and 1812. After reading his 1801 book *Disquisitiones arithmeticae* (Investigations in arithmetic), Germain sent him her proof of an unsolved problem. Worried that Gauss would not seriously consider her work if he knew she was a woman, she signed her letter Monsieur Le Blanc. Gauss corresponded with "Le Blanc" for three years before learning the mathematician's true identity.

In 1807 Germain learned that the French army was planning to invade the German city Brunswick, where Gauss lived. Recalling how Archimedes was killed by a soldier while working on his mathematics, she feared that Gauss would die the same way. At her request, General Joseph-Marie Pernety, a friend of Germain's father, sent a French military officer to Gauss's home to remove him from danger. When Gauss learned that Mademoiselle Germain ("Mademoiselle" means "Miss" in French) who saved his life was the true identity of Monsieur Le Blanc, he wrote her a long letter of thanks and became an even stronger supporter of her development as a mathematician. In 1810, when Gauss was honored by *l'Institut de France* (the Institute of France), Germain and the institute's secretary bought him a pendulum clock that he treasured for the rest of his life. Although they never met in person, Germain and Gauss maintained a lifelong friendship.

Sophie Germain Prime Numbers

One of the ideas that Germain, Legendre, and Gauss discussed was the concept of a prime number—a whole number greater than 1 that cannot be divided by any other positive number except itself and 1. For example, 13 is a prime number because the only ways to divide it without getting a remainder are $13 \div 13 = 1$ or $13 \div 1 = 13$. Numbers like 14 and 15 are not prime numbers because $14 \div 2 = 7$ and $15 \div 3 = 5$. The first several prime numbers are 2, 3, 5, 7, 11, 13, 17, and 19. This list continues forever because there are infinitely many prime numbers.

Germain investigated a special type of prime number that has come to be named in her honor. A prime number p is called a Sophie Germain prime if $2p + 1$ is also a prime number. Some examples are 2 (since $2 \times 2 + 1 = 5$ is prime), 3 (since $2 \times 3 + 1 = 7$ is prime), and 5 (since $2 \times 5 + 1 = 11$ is prime). The prime number 7 is not a Sophie Germain prime because $2 \times 7 + 1 = 15$ is not prime. With the encouragement and assistance of Legendre and Gauss, Germain discovered many properties of this class of prime numbers. Almost 200 years later, mathematical researchers are still studying Sophie Germain primes. These numbers have applications in cryptography for creating secure digital signatures and in number theory, where they are closely related to Mersenne primes, the

Prime number p	$2p + 1$	Is p a Sophie Germain prime?
2	$2 \times 2 + 1 = 5$	Yes, because 2 and 5 are prime.
3	$2 \times 3 + 1 = 7$	Yes, because 3 and 7 are prime.
5	$2 \times 5 + 1 = 11$	Yes, because 5 and 11 are prime.
7	$2 \times 7 + 1 = 15$	No, $15 \div 3 = 5$ so 15 is not prime.
11	$2 \times 11 + 1 = 23$	Yes, because 11 and 23 are prime.
13	$2 \times 13 + 1 = 27$	No, $27 \div 3 = 9$ so 27 is not prime.
17	$2 \times 17 + 1 = 35$	No, $35 \div 5 = 7$ so 35 is not prime.

© Infobase Publishing

A prime number p is a Sophie Germain prime if $2p + 1$ is also prime.

largest known prime numbers. Using computers, researchers have discovered millions of Sophie Germain primes, including one that is more than 34,000 digits long.

Fermat's Last Theorem

Germain made her discoveries about prime numbers while working on Fermat's Last Theorem, the most famous problem in number theory. For thousands of years, mathematicians had known that there were infinitely many sets of positive integers such as $x = 3$, $y = 4$, and $z = 5$ that satisfied the equation $x^2 + y^2 = z^2$. In the 1630s French mathematician Pierre de Fermat claimed that no integers satisfied the equation $x^n + y^n = z^n$ if the exponent n was greater than two. After he died, mathematicians were able to prove all the theorems that he stated except this one, so it became known as Fermat's Last Theorem. Around 1660 Fermat proved that this equation had no solutions if the exponent was $n = 4$. In 1738 Swiss mathematician Leonhard Euler proved that no solutions existed when $n = 3$. By 1800 these were the only two exponents for which Fermat's Last Theorem was known to be true.

In her first letter to Gauss, Germain sent him her proof of Fermat's Last Theorem when $n = p - 1$, where p is a prime number of the form $p = 8k + 7$. She thought she had proven that this famous theorem was true for infinitely many values of n such as $n = 6, 22$, 30, and 46. Although her proof was not correct, Gauss complemented her for her novel approach and encouraged her to continue working on the problem.

In the early 1820s, after working on the problem for more than 15 years, she made a significant discovery, which became known as Germain's theorem. Researchers had divided Fermat's Last Theorem into two cases: when none of the integers x, y, or z were divisible by n, and when one of x, y, and z was divisible by n. In her theorem, Germain identified two conditions under which the first case of the theorem was true. She demonstrated that these conditions work for all odd primes less than 100. She further explained how these conditions work for all odd Sophie Germain primes.

Her theorem was the most significant progress on this famous problem since it was first stated. In 1823 Legendre formally announced Germain's theorem to the mathematical community in a paper that he presented to the French Académie des Sciences (Academy of Sciences) an organization whose members included the best scientists and mathematicians in the country. He also included her theorem in a supplement to the second edition of his book *Essai sur le théorie des nombres*, the book that had sparked her first letter to him.

By generalizing the concept of Sophie Germain primes, Legendre was able to extend Germain's results to all odd primes less than 197. In 1908 American mathematician L. E. Dickson further generalized Germain's work to all odd primes less than 1,700. Germain's strategy was so effective that mathematicians continued to pursue it, achieving new results as late as 1991, only three years before English mathematician Andrew Wiles finally proved Fermat's last theorem.

Vibrating Surfaces

In addition to her important work in number theory, Germain made significant contributions to the mathematical explanations of vibrating or elastic surfaces. In 1808 German physicist Ernst F. F. Chladni visited Paris, giving demonstrations of a scientific phenomenon that was well known yet unexplained. He would sprinkle some fine sand on a thin, flat, circular sheet of glass or metal, and then rub a violin bow against the edge of the sheet. This caused the sand particles on the vibrating surface to align themselves into well-defined curves called Chladni Figures. The shape and number of curves could be varied by stroking the bow in different ways. These scientific demonstrations could be repeated with predictable and consistent outcomes, but no one could explain why the particular patterns formed the way they did.

The French emperor Napoléon Bonaparte, well educated in mathematics and science, was so fascinated by these patterns of vibration that in 1809 he asked mathematician Pierre-Simon Laplace to organize a competition to discover the mathematical explanation for them. The competition was sponsored and judged by the Academy of Sciences. The grand prize, a medal made from a kilogram of gold, would be awarded to the winner at a celebration at the conclusion of the two-year competition.

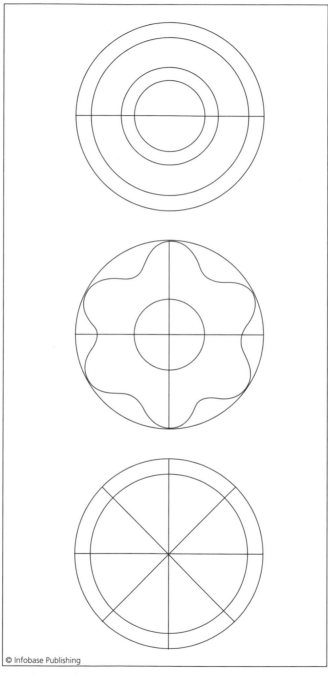

Germain won the grand prize in a competition sponsored by France's Academy of Sciences for her analysis of the theory of elasticity that explained why sand formed predictable patterns on vibrating surfaces.

Germain and many mathematicians throughout Europe started doing experiments to develop the equations that explained the patterns of vibration. Lagrange, who was one of the judges, predicted that no one would be able to solve the problem because the mathematics to explain it had not yet been discovered. When the two-year deadline arrived, Germain's research paper was the only entry in the competition. Although her basic approach to explaining why the patterns occurred was correct, there were some mistakes in her mathematical calculations. The judges decided to extend the competition until October 1813.

Lagrange helped Germain correct her mathematical errors and create a partial differential equation that more accurately described the patterns of the vibrations. When the second deadline arrived, her revised paper was again the only entry. This time, her theory based on Lagrange's equation more closely agreed with the well-known experimental results in a number of situations, but her explanation did not fully explain the phenomenon of vibrating surfaces. She had also incorrectly used a technique of double integrals that she did not fully understand and had not shown how she obtained Lagrange's equation from physical principles. The judges awarded her an honorable mention and extended the contest deadline for an additional two years.

In 1815 Germain presented a third paper addressing vibrations of general curved surfaces as well as flat surfaces. Although her work did not fully explain the pattern of vibrations in all cases, the judges were impressed with the originality and the sophistication of her theory, and they awarded her the grand prize, their *prix extraordinaire* (special prize). She did not appear at the award ceremony on January 8, 1816, to receive her gold medal, possibly because she was unaccustomed to being the center of attention in a large public gathering.

In 1821 at her own expense Germain published her enlarged and improved theory titled "Remarques sur la nature, les bornes et l'étendue de la question des surfaces élastiques et equation générale de ces surfaces" (Remarks on the nature, limits, and extent of the question of elastic surfaces and general equation of these surfaces). Although the theory was still incomplete and the paper included mathematical errors, it advanced the scientific dialogue and stimulated others to continue their work. In this paper she stated her law for the general vibrating elastic surface given by the fourth-degree partial differential equation

$$N^2\left[\frac{\partial^4 \rho}{\partial x^4} + 2\frac{\partial^4 \rho}{\partial x^2 \partial y^2} + \frac{\partial^4 \rho}{\partial y^4} - \frac{4}{S^2}\left(\frac{\partial^2 \rho}{\partial x^2} + \frac{\partial^2 \rho}{\partial y^2}\right)\right] + \frac{\partial^2 \rho}{\partial t^2} = 0.$$

In this equation, N represents the thickness of the surface, S is a measure of the surface's curvature, t represents time, x and y are the coordinates of a point on the surface, and p represents the amplitude of the vibration. Augustin-Louis Cauchy praised the paper, stating that it would earn the author lasting fame. Claude Navier, who was also researching the theory of vibrations, complimented her work for the complexity of the methods she employed.

In 1822 Jean-Baptiste Joseph Fourier, the permanent secretary of the Academy of Sciences, arranged for Germain to attend meetings of the academy and of its parent organization, the Institute of France. She became the first woman who was not married to a member to earn these privileges, which provided her greater access to discussions of current research and more opportunities to meet with leading French mathematicians.

During the next 10 years Germain continued to develop her theories and wrote three additional papers on the subject of vibrations of surfaces. In 1825 she submitted to the Institute of France a paper titled "Mémoire sur l'emploi de l'épaisseur dans la théorie des surfaces élastiques" (Memoir on the function of thickness in the theory of elastic surfaces). In this paper she explained how flat surfaces of various thicknesses vibrated differently. The paper contained some mathematical errors and was ignored by the mathematicians who read it. Fifty-five years later, it was rediscovered and was published in 1880 in the French *Journal de mathématiques pures et appliqués* (Journal of pure and applied mathematics).

Germain's 1828 paper "Examen des principes qui peuvent conduire à la connaissance des lois de l'équilibre et du movement des solides élastiques" (Investigation of the principles that may lead to an understanding of the laws of equilibrium and the movement of elastic solids) appeared in *Annales de chimie et de physique* (Annals of chemistry and physics). In this article she responded to Siméon-

Denis Poisson, who had criticized her work and had published a competing theory explaining the phenomenon of vibration at the molecular level. Germain defended her theory and offered her opinion that the purpose of mathematical investigation was to explain phenomena in mathematical terms without providing a theory for the underlying causes. For the next two decades mathematicians favored Poisson's molecular theory of vibration, but the modern theory of elasticity is based on the equations Germain and Lagrange derived.

In 1830 Germain wrote her final paper on vibrating surfaces. "Mémoire sur la courbure des surfaces" (Memoir on the curvature of surfaces) was published in the German *Journal für die reine und angewandte Mathematik* (Journal of pure and applied mathematics). In this paper she summarized her entire theory of vibrating surfaces and explained the concept of the mean curvature of a surface, which she had developed in the course of her research. The notion of curvature of a surface generalizes the concept of the curvature of a two-dimensional curve. Gauss had introduced a measure known as Gaussian total curvature in which he multiplied the maximum and minimum curvatures at each point on a surface. Germain modified this idea, taking the average of the maximum and minimum curvatures at each point. Her mean curvature provided a measure that was more useful for applications to elasticity theory. Mathematicians studying differential geometry continue to use this concept in their research.

Philosophical Writings

In addition to her work in mathematics, Germain wrote essays on philosophical themes. Two of these papers, a short biography, and a selection of some of her letters to other mathematicians were published in 1879 under the title *Oeuvres philosophiques de Sophie Germain* (Philosophical works of Sophie Germain). In the first paper, titled "Pensées diverses" (Diverse thoughts), Germain presented brief descriptions of several topics in science, her evaluation of the contributions of prominent mathematicians and scientists, and her personal opinions on various subjects. The second paper "Considérations générales sur l'état des sciences et des lettres"

(General considerations on the state of the sciences and letters) discussed the purposes, methods, and cultural importance that the sciences, philosophy, literature, and the fine arts share in common. Auguste Comte praised the essay as a scholarly development of the theme of the unity of thought.

In 1829 doctors determined that Germain had breast cancer, but the illness did not prevent her from completing additional work. During her final two years she composed her last paper on the curvature of surfaces and continued to correspond with other mathematicians and scientists. She wrote a short paper, "Note sur la manière dont se composent les valeurs de y et z dans l'équation $4(x^p - 1) / (x - 1) = y^2 \pm pz^2$ et celles de Y' et Z' dans l'équation $4(x^p - 1)/(x - 1) = Y'^2 \pm pZ'^2$" (Note on the manner by which one composes the values of y and z in the equation $4(x^p - 1)/(x - 1) = y^2 \pm pz^2$ and those of Y' and Z' in the equation $4(x^p - 1)/(x -1) = Y'^2 \pm pZ'^2$). The paper appeared in 1831 in the *Journal für die reine und angewandte Mathematik* (also known as *Crelle's Journal*). Gauss arranged for her to receive an honorary degree in mathematics from the University of Göttingen in Germany. Unfortunately, Germain died on June 26, 1831, at the age of 55, before the ceremony could be scheduled.

Conclusion

Sophie Germain made significant and lasting contributions to two areas of mathematics—elasticity and number theory. Building on the concepts that she developed in her prize-winning paper, mathematicians have fully developed a theory of elasticity that correctly explains the phenomenon of vibrating surfaces. The concept of mean curvature of a surface that she introduced in the process continues to be used by geometers. Number theorists recognize Germain's theorem as one of the significant milestones in the 350 years that it took to prove Fermat's Last Theorem. They continue to compete to see whose computer can break the record for discovering the largest Sophie Germain prime.

Three landmarks in Paris honor Germain's memory. A commemorative plaque on the house in which she died at 13 rue de Savoie marks the location as an historical landmark. In her honor the citizens of Paris named a street—Rue Sophie Germain—and a high school—École Sophie Germain.

FURTHER READING

Dalmedico, Amy Dahan. "Sophie Germain." *Scientific American* 265, no. 6 (1991): 116–122. Article with both biographical and mathematical content for scientifically literate audience.

Dauben, Joseph. "Review of 'Sophie Germain: An Essay in the History of the Theory of Elasticity' by Louis L. Bucciarelli and Nancy Dworsky." *American Mathematical Monthly* 92 (1985): 64–70. Article in mathematics journal providing a detailed description of her work on vibrating plates with some biographical information.

Gray, Mary W. "Sophie Germain (1776–1831)." In *Women of Mathematics: A Biobibliographic Sourcebook*, edited by Louise S. Grinstein and Paul J. Campbell, 47–56. New York: Greenwood, 1987. Biographical profile with an evaluation of her mathematics and an extensive list of references.

James, Ioan. "Sophie Germain." In *Remarkable Mathematicians from Euler to von Neumann*, 47–58. Washington, D.C.: Mathematical Association of America, 2003. Brief biography and description of her mathematics.

Kramer, Edna E. "Germain, Sophie." In *Dictionary of Scientific Biography*, vol. 5, edited by Charles C. Gillispie, 375–376. New York: Scribner, 1972. Encyclopedic biography including a detailed description of her mathematical writings.

Kramer, Jennifer. "Sophie Germain 1776–1831 French Number Theorist." In *Notable Mathematicians from Ancient Times to the Present*, edited by Robin V. Young, 201–203. Detroit, Mich.: Gale, 1998. Brief but informative profile of Germain and her work.

O'Connor, J. J., and E. F. Robertson. "Marie-Sophie Germain." In "MacTutor History of Mathematics Archive." University of Saint Andrews. Available online. URL: http://www-groups. dcs.st-andrews.ac.uk/~history/Mathematicians/Germain.html. Accessed on March 6, 2003. Online biography from the University of Saint Andrews, Scotland.

Osen, Lynn M. "Sophie Germain." In *Women in Mathematics*, 83–93. Cambridge, Mass.: MIT Press, 1974. Biographical sketch of Germain and her work.

Perl, Teri. "Sophie Germain." In *Math Equals: Biographies of Women Mathematicians + Related Activities*, 62–81. Menlo Park, Calif.: Addison-Wesley, 1978. Biography accompanied by exercises related to her mathematical work.

Reimer, Luetta, and Wilbert Reimer. "Mathematics at Midnight: Sophie Germain." In *Mathematicians Are People, Too, Stories from the Lives of Great Mathematicians*, 90–97. Parsippany, N.J.: Seymour, 1990. Life story with historical facts and fictionalized dialogue, intended for elementary school students.

Riddle, Larry. "Sophie Germain and Fermat's Last Theorem." Agnes Scott College. Available online. URL: http://www.agnesscott.edu/lriddle/women/germain-FLT/SGandFLT.htm. Accessed on July 1, 2004. Online article detailing Germain's contributions to the solution of this famous problem.

Smith, Sanderson M., and Greer Lleaud. "Sophie Germain." In *Notable Women in Mathematics: A Biographical Dictionary*, edited by Charlene Morrow and Teri Perl, 62–66. Westport, Conn.: Greenwood, 1998. Short biography of Germain.

2

Carl Friedrich Gauss

(1777–1855)

Carl Friedrich Gauss, a child prodigy who became the leading mathematician of the 19th century, contributed to almost every branch of mathematics and physics.
(Courtesy of AIP Emilio Segrè Visual Archives, Brittel Book Collection)

"Prince" of Mathematics

Carl Friedrich Gauss (pronounced GOWSE) was the leading mathematician of the 19th century. His book *Disquisitiones arithimeticae* (Investigations in arithmetic) unified the discipline of number theory. During the first 10 years of his 60-year career, he proved the fundamental theorem of arithmetic, the fundamental theorem of algebra, the law of quadratic reciprocity, and the constructability of regular polygons. He developed the method of least squares and the technique of Gaussian curvature. His ideas influenced data analysis, differential geometry, potential theory, statistics, calculus, matrix theory, ring theory, and complex function theory. As a physical scientist he made significant contributions to astronomy, geodesy, magnetism, and electricity. This "Prince of Mathematics" is considered one of the three greatest mathematicians who ever lived.

Child Prodigy

Johann Friedrich Carl Gauss was born on April 30, 1777, in Brunswick, Germany. From an early age he referred to himself as Carl Friedrich Gauss and throughout his professional life he signed his research papers and his correspondence with this name. Gerhard Diederich Gauss, his father, worked as a gardener, as a bricklayer, and as a foreman on a canal, while Dorothea Benz Gauss, his mother, worked as a maid. Gauss had one sibling, a half brother from his father's first marriage.

As a very young child Gauss showed signs of brilliance. He taught himself to read at the age of two by sounding out the letters in each word. When he was three, he discovered and corrected a mistake in his father's calculation of the weekly payroll for his workers. As a 10-year-old student he surprised his teacher Mr. Büttner when he mentally determined the sum of the numbers $1 + 2 + 3 + \ldots + 98 + 99 + 100$ by grouping them into 50 pairs that each totaled 101 to produce the result $50 \times 101 = 5{,}050$. Gauss showed the depth of his insight by explaining to his teacher how this technique could be used to sum any list of equally spaced numbers (called an arithmetic

$$\sum_{k=1}^{n} k = \frac{n(n+1)}{2} \qquad \text{When } n = 100,$$

$$\sum_{k=1}^{100} k = 1 + 2 + 3 + \cdots + 98 + 99 + 100 = \frac{100(101)}{2} = 5{,}050$$

While adding the numbers from 1 to 100 at the age of 10, Gauss rediscovered this classic formula for summing the terms of an arithmetic series.

series) by adding the first and last terms together then multiplying this sum by half the number of terms.

Büttner was one of several individuals who recognized Gauss's mathematical aptitude and took a special interest in this gifted young man. He lent Gauss additional books to study and convinced his parents to allow him to investigate advanced ideas after school with a tutor, Martin Bartels, who later became a mathematics professor at the University of Kazan. During Gauss's high school years E. A. W. Zimmerman, a mathematics professor at Caroline College, provided additional instruction and in 1791 introduced him to the duke of Brunswick, Karl Wilhelm Ferdinand. Impressed by his mathematical talents, the duke became Gauss's patron, paying for his college education and providing him a stipend for 15 years, enabling him to concentrate on his mathematical research.

Least Squares and Quadratic Reciprocity

In 1792, at the age of 15, Gauss enrolled as a student at Caroline College in Brunswick, where he spent three productive years. He developed two methods for calculating the square root of a number accurately to 50 decimal places. He investigated systems of geometry in which Euclid's parallel postulate did not hold and determined many properties that would be true in such non-Euclidean geometries. His natural ability to make rapid calculations with large sets of numbers enabled him to make two other discoveries that were so significant that either one of them would have solidly established his reputation within the mathematical community.

While studying how changes in individual values affected the average of a set of data, Gauss developed the method of least squares. For a set of data points plotted on a graph, this numerical technique provides a systematic way to find the line or curve that passes as close as possible to the collection of points. One of the most important techniques of data analysis, Gauss's method of least squares is frequently used in statistics and in all scientific fields. The method of least squares is particularly useful when working with data that might include errors due to inaccurate measurements or natural variations.

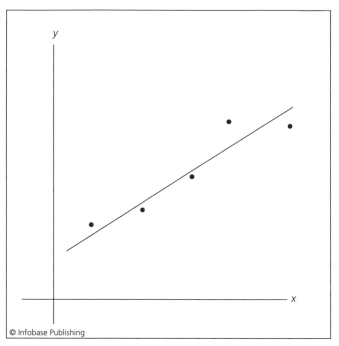

© Infobase Publishing

As a college student Gauss discovered the method of least squares that enables one to fit a regression line to a set of data points.

Gauss also discovered a deep and significant relationship between perfect squares—numbers such as $49 = 7^2$ and $100 = 10^2$ that can be written as integers raised to the second power—and prime numbers—numbers such as 2, 3, 5, and 7 that cannot be divided by any other positive integers except themselves and 1. He noticed that the prime numbers 3 and 13 could be combined to make many perfect squares either by starting with 13 and adding a number of 3s such as

$$13 + 3 \times 4 = 25 = 5^2 \text{ and } 13 + 3 \times 12 = 49 = 7^2$$

or by starting with 3 and adding a number of 13s such as

$$3 + 13 \times 6 = 81 = 9^2 \text{ and } 3 + 13 \times 22 = 289 = 17^2.$$

He also observed that the prime numbers 3 and 7 could be combined to make perfect squares by starting with 7 and adding a number of 3s such as

$$7 + 3 \times 6 = 25 = 5^2 \text{ and } 7 + 3 \times 19 = 64 = 8^2$$

but no perfect squares could be made by starting with 3 adding any number of 7s. He further noticed that for the prime numbers 3 and

5, it was not possible to make perfect squares by starting with 3 and adding a number of 5s or by starting with 5 and adding a number of 3s.

Gauss discovered a pattern that determined whether two odd prime numbers could be combined to make perfect squares in both ways, in one way, or not at all. He saw that the key was to notice what happened when both prime numbers were divided by 4. If the prime numbers p and q both had a remainder of 3, then there were perfect squares of one form but not the other. If p or q or both had a remainder of 1, then there were perfect squares of both forms or of neither form. Number theorists had been trying to prove this law of quadratic reciprocity for 50 years. Leonhard Euler in 1783 and Adrien Marie Legendre in 1785 had provided important pieces of the proof. Gauss's detailed mathematical argument in 1795, completed just months before his 18th birthday, finally established the important theorem.

University Years

After graduating from Caroline College in 1795, Gauss enrolled at the University of Göttingen, intending to pursue a degree in either mathematics or philology, the study of languages. In 1796 he determined that it was possible to construct a regular heptadecagon—a polygon with 17 equal sides and 17 equal angles—using a ruler and compass. From related results that he proved about the roots of cyclotomic polynomials, he developed the general geometrical result that a ruler-and-compass construction of a regular n-gon was possible if n could be written as a power of 2 times a product of distinct Fermat primes—prime numbers of the form $2^{2^k} + 1$. Zimmerman announced Gauss's proof of this result in the "New Discoveries" section of the June 1796 issue of the journal *Intellegenzblatt der allgemeinen Litteraturzeitung* (Intellectual magazine of general literature). Gauss's success solving this classic problem that had puzzled mathematicians for more than 2,000 years convinced him to devote all his efforts to mathematics. He considered this discovery one of his greatest achievements and requested that a regular 17-gon be engraved on his tombstone.

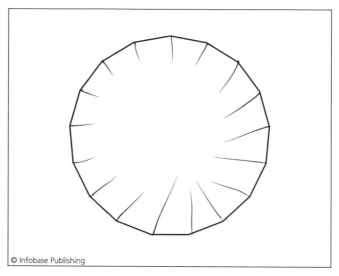

© Infobase Publishing

Gauss's construction of the regular 17-sided polygon convinced him to pursue a career in mathematics.

During his three years at the University of Göttingen, Gauss discovered proofs of many classic conjectures and developed new proofs of well-known results. He gave the first proof of the fundamental theorem of arithmetic—the principle that each positive integer can be written as a product of prime numbers in only one way. He rediscovered results about the arithmetic-geometric mean and the binomial theorem. Later in life he recalled that during this period of years ideas came to him so fast that he had difficulty writing them all down.

In 1798 Gauss transferred to the University of Helmstedt, a larger institution whose more extensive mathematical library provided him greater access to both classic and current mathematical research results. A year later, he completed his studies and earned a Ph.D. in mathematics under the nominal direction of Johann Friedrich Pfaff. In his dissertation, titled "Demonstratio nova theorematis omnem functionem algebraicam rationalem integram unius variabilis in factores reales primi vel secundi gradus resolvi posse" (A new proof that every rational integral function of one variable can be resolved into real factors of the first or second degree), he gave the first complete proof of the fundamental theorem of algebra. Many mathematicians, including Sir Isaac Newton, Leonhard Euler, and Joseph-Louis Lagrange, had unsuccessfully attempted to prove this basic principle concerning the factors of a polynomial.

Disquisitiones arithmeticae (Investigations in arithmetic)

Gauss did most of his early research in the area of number theory—the branch of mathematics that deals with integers and the properties of arithmetic. He called number theory "the queen of mathematics" because he considered it to be the first and most important part of the discipline. In 1801 he published his work in the book *Disquisitiones arithmeticae* (Investigations in arithmetic). In seven chapters he systematically summarized the work of earlier mathematicians, gave his solutions to some of the most difficult problems in the field, and presented new concepts and challenges that gave direction to future researchers in number theory. The work included new material on quadratic forms, congruent integers, the distribution of prime numbers, and modular equations, as well as the construction of the regular polygon with 17 sides, and his proofs of the law of quadratic reciprocity, the fundamental theorem of arithmetic, and the fundamental theorem of algebra. Gauss dedicated the book to Duke Karl Wilhelm Ferdinand in appreciation for his support and encouragement.

Immediately upon its publication, leading mathematicians throughout Europe praised the work as a masterpiece. In a letter to Gauss, Lagrange wrote that this achievement had raised him to the ranks of the best mathematicians in Europe. Belgium's Lejeune Dirichlet carried a copy of *Disquisitiones arithmeticae* with him in all his travels and slept with it under his pillow. The work unified number theory and firmly established it as an important area of mathematical research. Although leading mathematicians praised the work, Gauss's concise, polished style of exposition, the rigor of his argumentation, and the advanced nature of the mathematics made his book inaccessible for most mathematicians until Dirichlet and others amplified and re-explained the material 50 years later.

Mathematicians today regard this book that is densely packed with elegant proofs of significant results from number theory as one of the greatest mathematics books ever written.

Astronomy

After completing the work on his number theory book, Gauss became interested in the field of astronomy. On New Year's Day, 1801, Father Giuseppe Piazzi, an astronomer at the Palermo Observatory in Sicily, Italy, discovered a new asteroid, which he named Ceres. Observing the asteroid's position in the sky for 41 days before it passed behind the Sun, he estimated that it would reappear on the other side of the Sun approximately 10 months later. Many mathematicians, scientists, and astronomers unsuccessfully attempted to determine the exact time and place when Ceres would again be visible. Using his method of least squares and just three of Piazzi's observations, Gauss produced an accurate equation for the orbit of Ceres. Without disclosing his techniques, he published his prediction in a paper titled "Neigung der Bahn der Ceres" (Inclination of the orbit of Ceres) in the September issue of the major German astronomical journal *Monatliche Correspondenz zur Beförderung der Erd- und Himmelskunde* (Monthly correspondence in support of geographical and astronomical knowledge). When astronomers observed the asteroid's reappearance on December 7th exactly where Gauss had predicted, this achievement established his reputation as an applied scientist.

This success drew Gauss into a lifelong involvement with astronomy. Between 1802 and 1808 he wrote 15 papers presenting his observations and theories on the orbits of planets, comets, and asteroids. These included his 1808 paper "Beobachtungen der Juno, Vesta und Pallas" (Observations of Juno, Vesta and Pallas) published in the *Monatliche Correspondenz*, in which he gave accurate equations for the orbits of three recently discovered asteroids. After Duke Ferdinand died in 1806, Gauss rejected offers from several universities to become a mathematics professor. In 1807 he accepted an appointment as Director of the Observatory at Göttingen University, a position that he held for 48 years. In this capacity he actively pursued research in theoretical astronomy until

1818, taught courses in mathematics and astronomy until 1854, and regularly published his astronomical observations until 1855.

Events in Gauss's personal life during the first decade of the 19th century affected him deeply. In 1805 he married Johanna Osthoff, the daughter of a local tanner. Before she died in 1809, the couple had three children Joseph, Wilhelmine (called Minna), and Ludwig (called Louis), whom they named after Guiseppe Piazzi, Wilhelm Olbers, and Ludwig Harding, the astronomers who discovered the asteroids Ceres, Pallas, and Juno. Gauss regarded his four-year marriage to his first wife as the only happy period of his life. A year after her death, Gauss married her best friend, Friederica Wilhelmine Waldeck, the daughter of a law professor at the University of Göttingen. They had three children, Eugene, Wilhelm, and Therese, but Gauss continued to feel a tremendous sense of loss over the deaths of his first wife and his patron, the duke. Although he wrote thousands of letters to professional colleagues during his career, he resisted forming deep friendships, did not have warm relationships with most of his children, and had no close friends during his lifetime.

In 1809 Gauss published his major work on astronomical theory, the two-volume book *Theoria motus corporum coelestium in sectionibus conicis solem ambientium* (Theory of the motion of celestial bodies revolving around the Sun in conic sections). The first volume explained the necessary mathematical background on differential equations and conic sections; the second volume explained how to use the method of least squares to determine the orbit of an asteroid, comet, moon, or planet. Astronomers regarded this work as an important contribution to the field because it provided a rigorous mathematical technique for determining planetary orbits without requiring any assumptions about whether the orbits were circular, elliptic, parabolic, or hyperbolic.

While most of the 65 books and papers that Gauss produced between 1802 and 1818 were in the area of astronomy, he also published a number of papers on the underlying mathematical theory and on other topics in mathematics. Most of his mathematical papers during this period appeared in the journal *Commentationes der Königliche Societät der Wissenschaften der Göttingen* (Commentaries of the Royal Society of Sciences at Göttingen). He introduced the topic of Gaussian sums in his 1808 paper "Summatio quarundam serierum singularium" (Question about the summation of a singular series). His 1812 paper "Disquisitiones generales circa seriem infinitam" (General investigations about infinite series) gave a rigorous treatment of infinite series and introduced the hypergeometric function. He contributed significant ideas to the developing area of potential theory in the 1814 paper "Theoria attractionis corporum sphaeroidicorum ellipticorum homogeneorum methodus nova tractata" (Theory of attraction of spherical elliptical homogeneous bodies treated by a new method). In the same year he made an important contribution to the topic of approximate integrals with "Methodus nova integralium valores per approximationem inveniendi" (New methods for finding the value of an integral by approximations). His 1816 paper "Bestimmung der Genauigkeit der Beobachtungen" (Determinations of the accuracy of observations) published in the journal *Zeitschrift für Astronomie* (Journal for astronomy) presented an analysis of statistical estimators.

Professional Controversies

Gauss's publication of *Theoria motus* in 1809 was surrounded by controversy. Three years earlier, Legendre had published the method of least squares in an appendix to his book *Nouvelles méthods pour la détermination des orbites des comètes* (New methods for the determination of the orbits of comets). He accused Gauss of stealing his ideas and presenting them as his own. For many years Legendre bitterly fought to have the priority of his work recognized and to be credited with the discovery of the method of least squares. Gauss maintained that he had discovered the technique while he was a college student and had used it to determine the orbit of Ceres, but he refused to produce his notes in support of his claim.

Similar controversies occurred repeatedly throughout Gauss's career. When Irishman William Rowan Hamilton announced his discovery of the noncommutative algebraic objects called quaternions, when Frenchman Augustin-Louis Cauchy published an important theorem about integrals of complex functions, and when German Carl Jacobi wrote about the repeating properties of elliptic functions, Gauss asserted that he had already made each of these discoveries years earlier but had not published them. When Janos Bolyai in Hungary and Nikolai Lobachevsky in Russia announced their discoveries of non-Euclidean geometries, Gauss claimed that he had reached the same conclusions during his years at Caroline College.

Gauss became entangled in these disputes because he was a perfectionist. His philosophical approach to mathematical research was to fully investigate a subject and refine the results before publishing his discoveries. Faithful to his personal motto "Few, but ripe," he repeatedly reworked his proofs, searching for more concise arguments and more elegant explanations. During his career he produced four proofs of the fundamental theorem of algebra and eight proofs of the law of quadratic reciprocity. Each mathematical paper and book that he published made important contributions, but his critics charged that his unwillingness to share his unpublished work with others created animosity within the mathematical community and may have slowed the progress of mathematical discovery.

For 18 years Gauss kept a diary in which he noted his mathematical discoveries as they first occurred to him. In this journal he made 146 entries, each briefly explaining a result he had discovered and the date on which it occurred. The first entry, dated March 30, 1796, recorded his discovery of how to construct a 17-sided regular polygon. This record of discoveries could have settled many disputes, but he did not permit anyone to read it until after he died. When his diary finally became public in 1898, this record of his achievements, corroborated by the thousands of letters that he wrote to other mathematicians during his lifetime, supported his claims to the disputed discoveries.

Geodesy and Differential Geometry

From 1818 to 1828 Gauss focused most of his efforts on geodesy, the science of land measurement and mapmaking, and the underlying mathematical theory of differential geometry, the branch of mathematics that deals with the study of curved surfaces. His initial interest in geodesy arose in connection with the necessity of determining the precise location of his observatory on the surface of Earth in order to make accurate measurements of heavenly bodies. In 1822 he won first prize in a competition sponsored by the Copenhagen Academy in Denmark for his research paper "Allgemeine Auflösung der Aufgabe: Die Theile einer gegebenen Fläche auf einer andern gegebenen Fläche so abzubilden, dass die Abbildung dem Abgebildeten in den Kleinsten Theilen, ähnlich wird" (General solution of the problem: To represent the image of a given surface onto another surface so the image is similar to the original in every detail) in which he presented the first general treatment of conformal mappings and introduced the preliminary ideas of the theory of isometric mappings. This paper, together with several later works, led to the Gauss-Krueger projection, a technique that enabled geographers to produce accurate flat maps of large sections of Earth's spherical surface. His major work on differential geometry was the 1827 paper "Disquisitiones generales circa superficies curves" (General investigations about curved surface) published in *Commentationes*. In this paper he summarized a century of work on differential geometry, introduced the concept now known as Gaussian curvature that used techniques from calculus to quantify the curvature of a surface, and proved his *theorema egregium* (remarkable theorem) that Gaussian curvature is preserved by isometric mappings of surfaces.

In 1820 England's King George IV commissioned Gauss to conduct a survey of Hanover, a 15,000-square-mile region in northern Germany that was then under the control of the British government. To enable his surveying team to make accurate measurements, he invented the heliotrope, an instrument that used lenses and mirrors to reflect the light of the Sun so that the device could be seen by an observer from a distance of three miles. He provided a mechanism to readjust the heliotrope every four minutes to account for the continually changing position of the Sun due to the rotation of Earth. In the 20 years that he worked on this project, he made thousands of measurements and performed over a million calculations. At the conclusion of the project he was disappointed that the maps he produced were useful for geographic and military purposes but not for land surveys and that the data he had collected during this study were not exact enough to calculate the radius of Earth as he had originally hoped.

Magnetism and Electricity

From 1828 to 1840, while working on the Hanover land survey and continuing to direct the Göttingen Observatory, Gauss's primary research focused on the theory of magnetism and electricity. In 1828, while attending *Naturforscherversammlung* (Meeting of nature researchers), a three-week scientific conference in Berlin, he met Wilhelm Weber, a young German physicist who was conducting experiments with electromagnets. The two entered into a productive seven-year research partnership. Together they designed and constructed a laboratory building at the University of Göttingen made entirely of nonmagnetic metals in which to perform their experiments. In 1833 they invented an electromagnetic telegraph and devised a code that enabled them to send messages at the speed of eight words per minute. They ran wires from the observatory to the laboratory one mile away and used this method of communication for a number of years. Their model did not lead to a commercial product because inventors Samuel Morse in America and Carl August von Steinheil in Switzerland more rapidly developed the telegraphs they had invented at about the same time. Gauss and Weber established the *Magnetischer Verein* (Magnetic Association), a worldwide network of observation points to measure the magnetic force on the surface of Earth and created a journal *Resultate aus den beobachtungen des Magnetischen Vereins in Jahre . . .* (Results from the observations of the Magnetic Association in the year . . .) to publish the research of its members annually from 1837 to 1842. Through this worldwide collaboration of scientists they produced in 1840 the *Atlas des Erdmagnetismus* (Atlas of geomagnetism) a map of the magnetic field on the surface of Earth.

Gauss contributed to the understanding of terrestrial magnetism, the magnetic forces at different places on the surface of Earth. He invented the bifilar magnetometer, an instrument that measures the strength of Earth's magnetic forces. His 1833 paper "Intensitas vis magneticae terrestris ad mensuram absolutam revocata" (Intensity of terrestrial magnetism by absolute measure revisited) published in *Commentationes* introduced the systematic use of absolute units for distance, mass, and time to measure nonmechanical quantities. In his 1839 paper "Allgemeine Theorie des Erdmagnetismus"

(General theory of geomagnetism) published in *Resultate*, he proved that there can be only two magnetic poles on Earth—a North Pole and a South Pole. He theoretically determined the location of the magnetic South Pole and concluded that it did not coincide with the geographic South Pole, the endpoint of the axis on which Earth spins. His 1840 paper "Allgemeine Lehrsätze in Beziehung auf die im verkehrten Verhältnisse des Quadrats der Entfernung wirkenden Anziehungs- und Abstossungskräfte" (General teachings on the relation of attracting and repelling forces when the square appears in an inverse relation) provided the first systematic treatment of potential theory as a mathematical topic. Gauss considered his work on potential theory and his method of least squares to be vital links connecting theoretical science to observable natural phenomena.

In 1835 Gauss made his most important contribution to electricity and magnetism when he developed the principle known as Gauss's law, which states that the electric flux through any closed surface is proportional to the net electric charge enclosed by the surface. His work on this property was not published until after his death. Gauss's law is one of the four Maxwell equations that present a unified electromagnetic theory. In recognition of the significance of this contribution, scientists have defined the gauss as a unit of measure of magnetic field in the cgs system.

Other Discoveries

In addition to his work on astronomy, geodesy, magnetism, and electricity, Gauss made contributions to other areas of science. He developed mathematical techniques for studying the flow of liquids. He did basic research on acoustics, the study of sound. In optics he wrote papers about the design of multiple lenses and invented a lens called the Gaussian eyepiece that is still used today.

In mathematics his contributions extend beyond his discoveries in number theory, geometry, differential geometry, complex function theory, and potential theory. He developed new techniques for solving differential equations. His work on curved surfaces contributed to the new field of topology. His discovery of the bell curve, the normal (or Gaussian) distribution, and hypergeometric functions advanced mathematical knowledge in the field of statistics. In matrix theory his introduction of the technique of Gaussian elimination enabled mathematicians to solve problems involving simultaneous linear equations. In ring theory his Gaussian integers—complex numbers whose real and imaginary parts are integers—remain a fundamental concept. When he was asked how he was able to make so many important discoveries, he replied that anyone who concentrated as hard and as long as he did could have done the same.

In his last years Gauss served his community at Göttingen University in additional ways. He supervised the mathematical research of several doctoral students, including Richard Dedekind and Bernhard Riemann, who both became accomplished mathematicians. Several times he served as the school's dean of the faculty. Using his knowledge of statistics and his ability to read newspapers in foreign languages, he made international investments for the "widow's fund" that provided financial support to the wives and families of deceased faculty members. Applying the same shrewd strategies to his own finances, he accumulated considerable personal wealth. On February 23, 1855, Gauss died in his sleep at his home in Göttingen at the age of 77.

Conclusion

Gauss defined mathematics in the 19th century and made significant contributions to many branches of physical science. His masterpiece, *Disquisitiones arithmeticae*, which presented his proofs of the law of quadratic reciprocity, the fundamental theorem of arithmetic, the fundamental theorem of algebra, and the construability of regular polygons, along with his work on quadratic forms and modular arithmetic established number theory as a unified and significant branch of mathematics. His development of the concept of Gaussian curvature provided a rigorous technique that remains central to differential geometry. His method of least squares has become an essential method of data analysis in all quantitative disciplines. Gauss's contributions to potential theory, statistics, calculus, matrix theory, ring theory, and complex function theory shaped those branches of mathematics during his lifetime and continue to be of lasting importance. Gauss's law is a major result in electromagnetic theory. His contributions to the determination of planetary obits in astronomy, the mapping of curved surfaces in geodesy, and the theory of terrestrial magnetism are central concepts and techniques within those branches of the physical sciences.

During his lifetime Gauss earned such an honored status for his unparalleled talents and his many significant contributions that his fellow mathematicians called him the "Prince of Mathematics." Like the ancient Greek Archimedes, Gauss solved almost every major problem in mathematics in his day, contributed to every existing branch of mathematics, and invented many practical instruments. Like the Englishman Sir Isaac Newton, he looked at classic problems in mathematics and science and found the deep truths that others had missed. In the history of mathematics, these three—Archimedes, Newton, and Gauss—are honored as the three greatest mathematicians who ever lived.

FURTHER READING

Bell, Eric T. "The Prince of Mathematics." In *Men of Mathematics*, 281–269. New York: Simon & Schuster, 1965. Chapter 14 presents an extensive biography and evaluation of his mathematical work in the era that he defined.

Bühler, W. K. *Gauss: A Biographical Study*. Berlin: Springer-Verlag, 1981. Book-length biography.

Dunnington, Guy Waldo. *Carl Friedrich Gauss, Titan Of Science: A Study of His Life and Work*. New York: Exposition Press, 1955. Book-length biography.

James, Ioan. "Carl Friedrich Gauss (1777–1855)." In *Remarkable Mathematicians from Euler to von Neumann*, 58–69. Washington, D.C.: Mathematical Association of America, 2003. Brief biography and description of his mathematics.

May, Kenneth O. "Gauss, Carl Friedrich." In *Dictionary of Scientific Biography*, vol. 5, edited by Charles C. Gillispie, 298–315. New York: Scribner, 1972. Encyclopedic biography including a detailed description of his mathematical writings.

O'Connor, J. J., and E. F. Robertson. "Johann Carl Friedrich Gauss." In "MacTutor History of Mathematics Archive."

University of Saint Andrews. Available online. URL: http://
www-groups.dcs.st-andrews.ac.uk/~history/Mathematicians/
Gauss.html. Accessed on March 17, 2003. Online biography,
from the University of Saint Andrews, Scotland.

Reimer, Luetta, and Wilbert Reimer. "The Teacher Who Learned
a Lesson: Carl Friedrich Gauss." In *Mathematicians Are People,
Too, Stories from the Lives of Great Mathematicians*, 98–105.
Parsippany, N.J.: Seymour, 1990. Life story with historical facts
and fictionalized dialogue, intended for elementary school students.

3
Mary Fairfax Somerville

(1780–1872)

Mary Fairfax Somerville used her knowledge of mathematics to write popular science books on astronomy, the physical sciences, geography, and microscopic structures.
(Library of Congress)

"Queen" of Nineteeth-Century Science

Mary Fairfax Somerville was one of Europe's leading women of mathematics and science in the 19th century. Lacking a formal education, she mastered advanced theories of mathematics and science through a lifelong commitment to self-study. She performed experiments to investigate the effects of the rays of the Sun on steel needles, vegetable juices, and chemically-treated paper. She wrote about comets and advocated for the education of women. Her major achievements were four books on astronomy, the physical sciences, geography, and microscopic structures. These popular works, widely distributed throughout Europe and America, made advanced scientific theories accessible to the general public. Her accomplishments as a writer in various fields of science earned her international recognition within the mathematical and scientific community.

Early Life in Scotland

Mary Fairfax was born on December 26, 1780. William George Fairfax, her father, served in the British Navy, eventually rising to the rank of vice admiral. While returning from London, England, where she saw her husband depart on one of his navy voyages, Margaret Charters Fairfax stopped to visit her sister Martha in Jedburgh, Scotland, and gave birth to Mary.

Although they had many distinguished relatives, including America's first president, George Washington, Mary's family lived a modest lifestyle on their father's navy salary. She spent her childhood in the seaside village of Burntisland, Scotland, with her sister Margaret, her brothers Samuel and Henry, and three other siblings who died as infants. Her father's advancements in rank provided additional advantages for the family, including the opportunity to receive an education.

In 1789 Mary's parents sent her to an exclusive school for girls in Musselburgh, where she received her only year of formal education. The headmistress, Miss Primrose, taught the students to practice good posture, learn proper manners, and memorize pages from Samuel Johnson's *Dictionary of the English Language*. Although Mary disliked the strict discipline, she learned to read and write in English and French and developed a lifelong interest in reading.

During her teenage years and into her twenties, Mary and her family spent each winter in Edinburgh, the capital of Scotland. For several months each year she attended different finishing schools to learn the skills that were expected of a cultured young lady in upper-class society—sewing, playing the piano, dancing, drawing, and painting as well as reading Latin and Greek. She enjoyed a variety of social events, including parties, balls, theater performances, and concerts, and in her circle of friends became known as the "Rose of Jedburgh."

Introduction to Mathematics

Mary's mathematical education was haphazard and sporadic. As a 13-year-old student at one of the finishing schools, she took her first formal arithmetic class and quickly mastered the rules of the subject. She became interested in algebra—the branch of mathematics that expressed the rules of arithmetic in general terms—after discovering a puzzle in a women's fashion magazine during a tea party. Algebra was not part of the curriculum at the finishing school, but her brother's tutor, Mr. Gaw, provided her with a limited explanation of some of the fundamentals of the subject. During a painting class at Alexander Nasmyth's Academy, Mary overheard the instructor advising a male student that to learn more about the theory of perspective he should study Euclid's *Elements*, a classic text on arithmetic and geometry. Because it was considered improper for a young lady to purchase such a book, she convinced Gaw to buy her a copy of *Elements*.

Knowing that her parents would not approve of her interest in mathematics, Mary studied by candlelight in her bedroom at night. When the maid complained to her father that the household supply of candles kept running out, her parents discovered her secret activities. Her mother thought that her interest in mathematics was shameful, and her father worried that it would cause her to become mentally ill, two societal attitudes that were prevalent throughout Europe at the time. Although they took away her copy of *Elements* and forbade her to read any math books, she continued to recite the definitions, theorems, and examples that she had memorized from the first six chapters and defiantly sought opportunities to continue her study of mathematics.

First Marriage and Independence

In her early twenties Fairfax became reacquainted with her distant cousin Samuel Greig, a captain in the Russian Navy who was completing a training assignment aboard her father's ship. In May 1804, when he was assigned to a position at the Russian embassy in London, the two cousins married. Although Greig was a well-educated professional, he felt that it was not important for women to be educated and did not encourage his wife's mathematical studies. She gave birth to two sons, Woronzow and William George, before her husband died in 1807. He left her a modest inheritance that provided a comfortable lifestyle, enabling her to further her education and pursue her interests in mathematics and science.

Through independent reading and study, Fairfax developed her skills in algebra, trigonometry, and geometry. This background in mathematics enabled her to read and understand books on astronomy and other branches of science. She lacked access to an institution of higher education for women and had limited contact with educated people who were willing to discuss the material she was reading. These obstacles, combined with her relatives' and friends' disapproval and discouragement, impeded her educational progress. After several years she found a sympathetic group of well-educated men who supported the idea of higher education for women.

William Wallace, a mathematics professor at the Royal Military College in Great Marlow, Scotland, was one colleague with whom Fairfax exchanged many letters. He encouraged her, gave her frequent advice, and suggested books for her to read. Following his counsel, she built a strong personal library and rapidly developed her mathematical talents. Wallace helped her to read through difficult books such as *Principia mathematica* (Principles of mathematics), in which English mathematician Sir Isaac Newton explained his theory of calculus, and the newly published *Mécanique céleste* (Celestial mechanics), in which French mathematician Pierre-Simon de Laplace explained the laws that governed the motions of the planets. With Wallace's encouragement, she regularly submitted her solutions to the challenging problems that appeared in each issue of the Scottish journal *Mathematical Repository*. In 1811 one of her published solutions won a silver medal.

Second Marriage and the Start of a Career in Science

In May 1812 Fairfax married her first cousin Dr. William Somerville, a military physician who served as the head of army hospitals in Scotland. Although Mary was born at his parent's house in Jedburgh, they had rarely met during the next 30 years. Unlike her first husband, Captain Greig, Dr. Somerville was very supportive of her interest in mathematics, science, and education. With his encouragement, she furthered her knowledge of Greek and became interested in the study of botany. Together, they read through books on geology and mineralogy.

In the next five years Somerville gave birth to four more children—Margaret, Thomas, Martha Charters, and Mary Charlotte. She took personal responsibility for the education of her five children (her son William George had died in 1814) teaching them in all subjects. In addition to her growing family responsibilities, she continued to develop her own mathematical and scientific abilities.

In 1816 the Somervilles moved to London, where they lived for the next 20 years. They attended popular scientific lectures at the Royal Institution and became well known in educated circles. They developed friendships with many English scientists, including astronomers John and Caroline Herschel, mathematician Charles Babbage, and astronomer Edward Parry, who later named a small island in the Arctic Ocean after Mrs. Somerville. These contacts provided her several opportunities to work as an assistant to some of England's leading scientists. The Somervilles frequently traveled to France, Switzerland, and Italy, where they developed lifelong friendships with mathematicians and scientists throughout Europe, friendships that provided her access to the most current discoveries and advances in all branches of mathematics and science.

In 1825 Somerville completed a series of physics experiments on the connection between magnetism and the rays of the Sun. Working in her garden, she focused sunlight on a steel sewing needle and observed that, after a period of time, the needle appeared to be magnetized. She described her discoveries in a research paper entitled "On the Magnetizing Power of the More Refrangible Solar Rays." Dr. Somerville, who had been elected as a Fellow of the Royal Society, the leading professional organization of scientists in England, presented his wife's paper at one of their meetings in 1826. The members of the Royal Society were impressed with her work and published her paper later that year in their journal *Philosophical Transactions*. The presentation and publication of her paper were both exceptional accomplishments. Only one other woman, Caroline Herschel, a German-born astronomer who discovered eight comets and created a catalogue of 2,500 stars, had ever had her research so honored by the Royal Society. Although the theory that Somerville proposed in her paper was eventually disproved by other scientists, the paper established her reputation as a skillful scientific writer.

Writing Her First Book

The success of this paper brought Somerville an invitation to write an astronomy book. In 1827 Lord Henry Brougham, a friend of the Somervilles, and an officer in the Society for the Diffusion of Useful Knowledge, wrote to Dr. Somerville, asking if his wife would be willing to create an English version of Laplace's *Mécanique céleste*. Although the society respected her as a woman who possessed a deep knowledge of mathematics and science and who had demonstrated strong abilities as a writer on technical subjects, they complied with the societal expectation that their correspondence should be addressed to her husband.

Somerville was confident that she could translate from French into English Laplace's classic work that summarized the discoveries of several generations of scientists and mathematicians on gravitational theory and the motions of the bodies in the solar system. Successfully explaining the sophisticated theories in a manner that made them more accessible to general audiences posed a greater challenge. She agreed to undertake the project under the condition that her work was to be done in secret so that, if she did not create an acceptable edition of the book, no one outside the society would know of her failure.

Somerville worked on this project for three years, transforming Laplace's technical mathematical arguments into simpler explanations. She created explanatory diagrams to illustrate various scientific principles, explained complicated theories in terms of simpler examples, and devised experiments that made the material easier to understand. Her husband assisted by obtaining library books and by copying by hand her many revisions of the manuscript.

When the book *The Mechanisms of the Heavens* was published in 1831, it exceeded the expectations of the members of the Society for the Diffusion of Useful Knowledge. Laplace complimented Somerville for her clear and accurate interpretations of the advanced mathematical and scientific theories. The Royal Society was so impressed with this book that they hired a sculptor to carve a bust of Somerville so that her statue could be located in a place of honor in their meeting room. All 750 copies of the first printing sold out in less than a year, and additional printings had to be made. The book quickly became a standard textbook for honor students at Cambridge University and was widely distributed in Great Britain and throughout Europe. The first portion of the book, in which she explained the necessary mathematical background, was also published separately in 1832 under the title *A Preliminary Dissertation to the Mechanisms of the Heavens.*

Second Book Brings Honors and Recognition

The success of this book led to another writing project. While spending the next year in Europe visiting with friends from the scientific community, Somerville completed most of the chapters of a second book entitled *The Connection of the Physical Sciences.* In this work she explained the theories of light, sound, heat, motion, electricity, magnetism, gravity, and astronomy and showed how these various physical phenomena were closely related to one another.

When *The Connection of the Physical Sciences* was published in 1834, it was a bigger success than *The Mechanisms of the Heavens* had been. Between 1834 and 1877, 10 editions of the book were printed in English, French, Italian, and Swedish, and sold throughout Europe as well as in America. The book was not only popular with general readers but was also useful to scientists. Astronomer John Couch Adams, who discovered Neptune, credited a passage in Somerville's book with inspiring him to look for this new planet near Uranus. The book helped to influence the European scientific community to begin to view the physical sciences as a unified field, rather than continue to think of each topic as a separate branch of science.

Upon the publication of her second book, Somerville received recognition from many scientific and governmental bodies. In 1835 she and Caroline Herschel became the first women to be elected to England's Royal Astronomical Society. In 1834 and 1835 she was honored with memberships in the Swiss Society of Physics and Natural History, the Irish Royal Academy, and the Bristol Philosophical and Literary Society. She was invited to meet England's Queen Adelaide, to whom she had dedicated the book, and Princess Victoria. The British Prime Minister, Sir Robert Peel, awarded her a generous civil pension of 200 pounds per year, an amount that was raised to 300 pounds per year when the Somervilles experienced some financial problems a few years later.

Somerville became a prominent figure in London's intellectual circles strongly supporting women's rights and the education of women. When John Stuart Mill submitted a petition to Parliament seeking to give women the right to vote, she was the first to sign it. She assisted women who showed promise in math and science, introducing them to scientists and mathematicians who were willing to help them. She significantly influenced the career of Ada Lovelace, the daughter of Lord and Lady Byron, by tutoring her in mathematics and introducing her to mathematician Charles Babbage, who involved her in his work with his Analytical Engine.

Somerville's fame and recognition did not distract her from her scientific work. In 1835, when Halley's Comet made its expected appearance streaking across the night skies of Europe, she was visiting Italy near the Collegio Romano (Roman College). She sought permission to use their observatory that housed one of the most powerful telescopes in Europe to view the famous comet that appears only once every 76 years. Her request was denied because women were not allowed to use the facilities of this monastery where men were trained for the priesthood. Despite this restriction, she wrote a lengthy essay titled "On Halley's Comet" that was published in the December 1835 issue of the popular science magazine *Quarterly Review*.

In 1835 Somerville designed and conducted a series of experiments to investigate some chemical properties of the rays of the

Sun. She discovered how different materials caused a range of chemical reactions when they were placed on paper treated with silver chloride and then exposed to the sunlight. The discoveries she made through these experiments revealed some of the basic chemical properties that eventually led to the development of photography. She wrote a research paper about her work and sent it to her colleague D. F. J. Arago, who read portions of the paper to a meeting of the French Academy of Sciences in 1836. Her paper entitled "Experiments on the Transmission of Chemical Rays of the Solar Spectrum Across Different Media" was published that year in the French scientific journal *Comptes rendus de l'Academie des Sciences* (Rendering of the accounts of the Academy of Sciences).

Move to Italy

In 1836, when Dr. Somerville's health problems required that he live in a warmer climate, the couple moved from London to Italy, where they lived for the rest of their lives. They became popular and respected members of the Italian mathematical and scientific community. Between 1840 and 1845, Somerville was elected to membership in six Italian scientific societies. Although in her sixties, she produced several unpublished papers, including a scientific essay on meteors, similar to her piece on Halley's Comet, and a mathematical paper titled "On Curves and Surfaces of Higher Orders." She also wrote two books titled *The Form and Rotation of the Earth* and *The Tides of the Ocean and Atmosphere*, which she did not attempt to publish.

Somerville also continued her scientific research designing and conducting a third series of experiments to study the effects of the Sun's rays. When she completed her analysis, John Herschel presented the results at a meeting of the Royal Society. A portion of her paper entitled "On the Action of Rays of the Spectrum on Vegetable Juices" appeared in 1845 in *Abstracts of the Philosophical Transactions of the Royal Society*.

At the age of 67, Somerville published *Physical Geography*, the first major work written in English to study the physical surface of Earth by investigating its land masses, climates, soils, and vegetation. This innovative book earned her wide international recognition, selling more copies than either of her first two published books. Printed in seven editions between 1848 and 1877, the popular book was widely used in European schools and universities for 50 years. England's Royal Geographical Society honored Somerville for this work by awarding her their 1869 Victoria Gold Medal. In recognition of this accomplishment, the American Geographical and Statistical Society and the Italian Geographical Society elected her to membership. Between 1853 and 1857, five other Italian scientific societies admitted her as a member, and several scientific organizations awarded her medals of achievement.

In 1869, at the age of 88, Somerville wrote two final books. In the two-volume work *On Molecular and Microscopic Science* she presented a summary of discoveries in biology, chemistry, and physics about the molecular form of matter and the microscopic structure of plants. English biologist Charles Darwin, who later became famous for his revolutionary ideas on the theory of evolution, provided some of the illustrations for the book. She also wrote a book-length account of her life and of the many influential and important people she had known. In 1873 her daughter Martha published portions of this autobiography under the title *Personal Reflections from Early Life to Old Age of Mary Somerville.*

Productive Life Comes to an End

Somerville outlived her husband, who died in 1860, four of her six children, and most of her friends and colleagues. She was almost deaf and had difficulty remembering events and people's names but her mathematical and scientific mind remained sharp. Even in her last days she continued to read math books for four or five hours each morning as she had done each day for the past 60 years

On November 29, 1872, Mary Fairfax Somerville died peacefully in her sleep at her home in Naples, Italy, at the age of 91. When she died, London's *Morning Post* newspaper called her the "Queen of Nineteenth Century Science" in recognition of her role as one of the most visible women in the European scientific community for so many years.

Several of England's educational institutions have preserved Somerville's legacy as an educated woman of mathematics and science. Shortly after her death, her children donated most of the books in her personal library to Ladies' College at Hitchin, now known as Girton College at Cambridge University. In 1879 Oxford University established Somerville College as one of its first two women's colleges. The Mary Somerville Scholarship at Oxford University enables talented young women to pursue an advanced education in mathematics.

Conclusion

Somerville's principal contributions to science were her four books on astronomy, the physical sciences, geography, and microscopic structures. These popular works made advanced scientific theories accessible to nonspecialists throughout the Western world. The second of these books, *The Connection of the Physical Sciences*, also influenced the European scientific community to begin to consider the physical sciences as a unified field rather than as a collection of unrelated branches of science. Although her experiments on solar rays and her paper on Halley's Comet were not significant scientific advances, they and her books gave compelling evidence that women were capable of understanding and contributing to the fields of mathematics and science. Her productive career as a self-taught woman helped to change the attitudes of many members of the scientific community who embraced her as a scientific colleague and honored her lifetime of work.

FURTHER READING

Moore, Patrick. "Mary Fairfax Somerville 1780–1872 Scottish-Born English Mathematics Writer." In *Notable Mathematicians from Ancient Times to the Present*, edited by Robin V. Young, 445–447. Detroit, Mich.: Gale, 1998. Brief but informative profile of Somerville and her work.

O'Connor, J. J., and E. F. Robertson. "Mary Fairfax Greig Somerville." In "MacTutor History of Mathematics Archive." University of Saint Andrews. Available online. URL: http://www-groups.dcs.st-andrews.ac.uk/~history/Mathematicians/Somerville.html. Accessed on February 23, 2004. Online biography, from the University of Saint Andrews, Scotland.

Osen, Lynn M. "Mary Fairfax Somerville." In *Women in Mathematics*, 95–116. Cambridge, Mass.: MIT Press, 1974. Biographical sketch of Somerville and her work.

Patterson, Elizabeth Chambers. "Mary Fairfax Greig Somerville (1780–1872)." In *Women of Mathematics: A Biobibliographic Sourcebook*, edited by Louise S. Grinstein and Paul J. Campbell, 208–216. New York: Greenwood, 1987. Biographical profile with an evaluation of her mathematics and an extensive list of references.

———. *Mary Somerville and the Cultivation of Science, 1815–1840.* Boston: Nijhoff, 1983. Book-length biography.

———. "Somerville, Mary Fairfax Greig." In *Dictionary of Scientific Biography*, vol. 12, edited by Charles C. Gillispie, 521–525. New York: Scribner, 1972. Encyclopedic biography including a detailed description of her mathematical writings.

Perl, Teri. "Mary Fairfax Somerville (1780–1872)." In *Math Equals: Biographies of Women Mathematicians + Related Activities*, 82–99. Menlo Park, Calif.: Addison-Wesley, 1978. Biography accompanied by exercises related to her mathematical work.

Reimer, Luetta, and Wilbert Reimer. "The Mystery of X and Y: Mary Somerville." In *Mathematicians Are People, Too, Stories from the Lives of Great Mathematicians, Volume Two*, 80–89. Parsippany, N.J.: Seymour, 1995. Life story with historical facts and fictionalized dialogue, intended for elementary school students.

Termaat, Barbara. "Mary Fairfax Greig Somerville." In *Notable Women in Mathematics: A Biographical Dictionary*, edited by Charlene Morrow and Teri Perl, 233–238. Westport, Conn.: Greenwood, 1998. Short biography of Somerville.

4

Niels Henrik Abel

(1802–1829)

Niels Henrik Abel introduced the concept of elliptic functions, proved the
impossibility of creating algebraic
formulas to solve all higher-degree
polynomial equations, and developed rigorous methods to determine
the convergence of infinite series.
(Courtesy of the Library of Congress)

Elliptic Functions

In the last 10 years of his brief 26-year life Niels Henrik Abel
(pronounced AH-bull) contributed significant ideas to the development of algebra, functional analysis, and the rigorous character of
the discipline of mathematics. As a college student he proved that
no formula existed to solve polynomial equations of degree five, a
question that had been unanswered for three centuries. He proved
that the general binomial theorem was valid for real and complex

exponents. In a memoir that one of the leading mathematicians in France misplaced, he introduced the concept of elliptic functions. His theorems and methods concerning the convergence of infinite series helped bring a level of rigor back to mathematical discourse.

Family Life and Education

Niels Henrik Abel was born on August 5, 1802, in Finnöy, a small island village off the southwestern coast of Norway. Sören Georg Abel, his Lutheran minister-father who had university degrees in theology and philosophy, served as pastor of Finnöy and the surrounding islands. His mother, Anne Marie Simonson, the daughter of a wealthy merchant and shipowner, was a talented pianist and singer. In 1804 the family moved to Gjerstad, where minister Abel succeeded his father as pastor and became involved in national politics, eventually serving two terms as a member of the Storting, Norway's parliament.

Abel received his early education from his father, who tutored him and his six siblings at home. In 1815 his parents sent him and his older brother to the Cathedral School, a private boarding school in the capital city of Christiania (now Oslo). Berndt Holmboe, who became his mathematics teacher in 1818, noticed his aptitude for the subject and introduced him to the writings of the leading mathematicians of Europe, including Sir Isaac Newton, Leonhard Euler, Pierre-Simon de Laplace, and Joseph-Louis Lagrange. Within a year he started to engage in independent research projects. Years later, he attributed the rapid development of his mathematical talents to reading the works of the masters rather than those of their pupils. When Abel's father died in 1820, Holmboe secured a scholarship, enabling him to complete his final year of studies.

In 1821, on the strength of his high scores on the mathematics portion of the entrance examination, Abel entered the University of Christiania, the only institution of higher learning at the time in Norway. After earning his degree, he intended to become a mathematics professor so that he could financially support his struggling family. Aware of his exceptional abilities and his destitute financial situation, the university provided a free dormitory room and the faculty contributed money from their own salaries to pay his tuition and other expenses. Christoffer Hansteen, professor of astronomy and applied mathematics, and Sören Rasmussen, the only professor of mathematics, directed his mathematical studies and provided additional financial support. Within a year he completed the basic coursework in general studies and devoted his attention full-time to original mathematical research.

Solvability of Algebraic Equations by Radicals

One line of independent mathematical research that Abel had been pursuing since 1820 involved the 300-year-old search for the quintic formula. Mathematicians had developed formulas to solve polynomial equations whose highest terms had degree 1, 2, 3, and 4. The simple formula $x = -\dfrac{b}{a}$ gave the solution to linear equations of the form $ax + b = 0$ and the quadratic formula $x = \dfrac{-b \pm \sqrt{b^2 - 4ac}}{2a}$ provided the solution to all second-degree equations of the form $ax^2 + bx + c = 0$. Mathematicians had also created formulas to solve third- and fourth-degree equations whose highest powered terms were x^3 or x^4 but had been unable to discover similar formulas for higher degree equations.

During his final year at the Cathedral School, Abel thought he had found the quintic formula to find the roots of any fifth-degree equation. He wrote a preliminary draft of a paper explaining his method and showed it to Holmboe and Hansteen. They forwarded his manuscript to Ferdinand Degan, professor of mathematics at the University of Copenhagen, Denmark, with the request that the Danish Academy publish their student's result. After reviewing Abel's work, Degan asked him to amplify his explanations and to illustrate his method with specific examples. While creating the examples, he discovered an error in his analysis and started to reconsider the question of whether such a formula was possible.

In December 1823, while at the University of Christiania, Abel proved that it was impossible to construct a quintic formula that solved all fifth-degree equations using only a finite number of additions, subtractions, multiplications, divisions, and extractions of roots, a method known as solving equations by radicals. At his own expense he published his proof in a brief pamphlet titled *Mémoire sur les équations algébriques où on démontre l'impossibilité de la résolution de l'équation générale du cinquième degré* (Memoir on algebraic equations demonstrating the impossibility of the resolution of the general equation of the fifth degree). The financial constraints that forced him to condense his argument to six pages made the reasoning in his proof difficult to follow. When he sent copies of the pamphlet to leading mathematicians throughout Europe early in 1824, the cryptic proof by a young, unknown student generated no responses. German mathematician Carl Friedrich Gauss, whose comments Abel was particularly intent on hearing, threw away the pamphlet without reading it.

Despite the memoir's failure to generate interest from any member of the European mathematical community, Abel continued to expand his research on the solution of equations by radicals and to try to get his work on the topic published. In 1826 an expanded explanation of his discovery titled "Beweis der Unmöglichkeit, algebraische Gleichungen von höheren Graden als dem vierten allgemein aufzulösen" (Proof of the impossibility of the general solution of algebraic equations of degree higher than the fourth) appeared in the first issue of the German mathematics quarterly *Journal für die reine und angewandte Mathematik* (Journal for pure and applied mathematics). In this paper he proved the more general result that it was impossible to construct an algebraic formula to solve all equations of any degree higher than four using only the four arithmetic operations and the extraction of roots. In his proof he developed the concept of an algebraic field extension, a key concept in the developing discipline of abstract algebra.

In the 1828 manuscript *Sur la résolution algébraique des equations* (On the algebraic resolution of equations), which was not published until after his death, Abel acknowledged the existence of an obscure 1799 proof by Italian mathematician Paolo Ruffini that there was no quintic formula. In honor of these two mathematicians, the important result that the general equation of degree n is not solvable by radicals if $n > 4$ is now known as the Abel-Ruffini theorem.

Abel recorded his final comments on the subject in the 1829 paper "Mémoire sur une classe particulière d'équations résolubles algébriquement" (Memoir on a particular class of equations that are algebraically resolvable) that appeared in the same journal as his 1826 paper. In this work he explained that if the roots of a polynomial equation satisfied a certain condition then the equation was solvable by radicals. Building on Abel's ideas, French mathematician Évariste Galois finished the analysis of the topic in 1831, specifying a complete set of conditions that determined whether or not an equation was solvable by radicals.

General Binomial Theorem

During his years at the University of Christiania, Abel worked on several other research projects. In 1823 he published three articles in *Magazin for Naturvidenskaben* (Magazine for the natural sciences), the Norwegian scientific journal that Hansteen had recently established. His first two papers on functional equations and integrals were not significant results, but his third paper titled "Opläsning afet Par Opgaver ved bjoelp af bestemte Integraler" (Solution of some problems by means of definite integrals) contained the first published solution of an integral equation. The paper addressed the motion of a point mass moving along a curve under the influence of a gravitational force.

In the summer of 1823 Rasmussen financed a trip enabling Abel to travel to Copenhagen to work with Degen and other Danish mathematicians. During this visit he met a young woman named Christine Kemp and became engaged to be married. Recognizing the benefits obtained through collaboration with talented colleagues, Abel submitted a collection of his manuscripts to the Norwegian government and requested that they provide him funds so he could travel to Europe to work with the leading mathematicians in France and Germany. The government awarded him a stipend to study the French and German languages in Norway for two years and the travel funds to visit Europe for the following two years.

In September 1825 Abel and four friends who were preparing for careers in medicine and geology departed for Germany. In Berlin he met August Leopold Crelle, the civil engineer who designed

Germany's first railroad system, who was working to establish the *Journal für die reine und angewandte Mathematik*. This German mathematics quarterly, which became known as *Crelle's Journal*, was the first scholarly periodical devoted exclusively to the publication of new mathematical research. Crelle vigorously promoted Abel's work, publishing 33 of his research papers in the journal, including seven articles in the first volume in 1826. In addition to Abel's memoir on the impossibility of solving the quintic equation, his papers in the quarterly journal's first four issues included "Untersuchungen

über die Reihe $\quad 1 + \dfrac{m}{1}x + \dfrac{m(m-1)}{1\cdot2}x^2 + \dfrac{m(m-1)(m-2)}{1\cdot2\cdot3}x^3 + \ldots$ "

(Examination of the series . . .). In this paper he gave the first proof of the binomial theorem for real and complex values of m showing that this infinite sum of terms equaled $(1 + x)^m$. This result generalized Newton's 1669 discovery that the binomial theorem was valid for all fractional exponents.

Elliptic Functions

In the spring of 1826 Abel and his companions traveled to Italy, Austria, Switzerland, and France. By the time they arrived in Paris it was July, the universities had dismissed for the summer, and most of the mathematicians he had hoped to visit had left for their vacations. In anticipation of their return he wrote a lengthy manuscript titled "Mémoire sur une propriété générale d'une classe très-étendue de fonctions transcendantes" (Memoir on a general property of a very extensive class of transcendental functions), which he hoped to present to the mathematicians at the Académie des Sciences (Academy of Sciences). In this treatise he provided a detailed explanation of his discoveries involving elliptic functions.

Abel had created elliptic functions as generalizations of the circular or trigonometric functions. French mathematician Adrien-Marie Legendre had been studying complicated elliptic integrals of

the form $\displaystyle\int_{0}^{x} \dfrac{dt}{\sqrt{\left(1 - K^2 t^2\right)\left(1 - t^2\right)}}$ that expressed the length of an arc

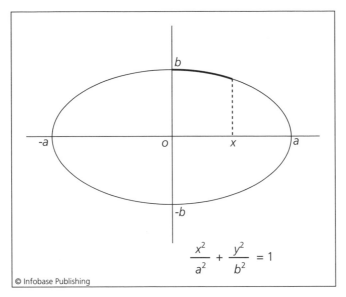

© Infobase Publishing

Abel discovered elliptic functions as inverses of the integrals associated with the arc length along an ellipse.

along an ellipse. Abel observed that on a circle, the simplest type of ellipse, where the integral $\arcsin(x) = \int_0^x \dfrac{dt}{\sqrt{1-t^2}}$ expressed the length of an arc, the inverse function, sin (x), had more elegant properties and was much easier to analyze than the corresponding integral. In a parallel manner he introduced the elliptic sine function, $sn(x)$, as the inverse of the elliptic integral. He successfully developed an extensive analysis of the properties of this and other elliptic functions.

One simple property that Abel established in this memoir was the doubly periodic nature of elliptic functions. All circular functions were known to be periodic, repeating their behaviors on a regular basis. The equation sin $(x + 2\pi)$ = sin (x) expresses the fact that the graph of the sine function repeats its values after every interval of length 2π. Abel discovered that every elliptic function $f(x)$ had two periods w and z for which $f(x + w) = f(x + z) = f(x)$. Abel's discovery of doubly periodic functions led him and other mathematicians to investigate the more general classes of functions now known as hyperelliptic functions and Abelian functions.

In his Paris memoir Abel also introduced the concept of the genus of an algebraic function when he proved that any sum of integrals of an algebraic function could be expressed as a fixed number of integrals of a particular form. That fixed number, known as the genus of the function, was a fundamental quantity that characterized the function and indicated many of its properties. German mathematician Carl Gustav Jacobi, who was also conducting research on elliptic functions, proclaimed that this important theorem, now known as Abel's theorem, was the greatest mathematical discovery of the era.

When Abel presented his memoir on elliptic functions to the Paris Academy in October 1826, Legendre and Augustin-Louis Cauchy were appointed as referees but never evaluated the work. Legendre claimed that he was unable to read the manuscript because the ink was too faint. Cauchy misplaced the treatise before he had the opportunity to read it.

Disappointed by the disregard that the French mathematicians showed for his work, almost out of money, and suffering the early symptoms of tuberculosis, Abel returned to Berlin for a few months. Although Crelle offered him the position of editor of his journal and promised to obtain for him a professorship at a German university, he returned home in May 1827. In Norway Abel had hoped to succeed Rasmussen as professor of mathematics at the University of Christiania, but Holmboe had accepted that position. He survived until the end of the year on a small stipend provided by the university and the money he earned tutoring. Early in 1828 he secured a substitute teaching position at the university and at the Norwegian Military Academy when Hansteen accepted a two-year grant to study Earth's magnetic field in Siberia.

During this time Abel continued his research on elliptic functions and wrote several articles for *Crelle's Journal*. He published the first half of his Paris memoir in September 1827 as "Recherches sur les functions elliptiques" (Research on elliptic functions). When Jacobi announced several new results about transformations of elliptic functions in 1828, Abel published the second half of his memoir under the same title and added a section explaining how Jacobi's results followed from his own work. During the next year he and Jacobi produced a series of papers responding to and extending each other's results. Before the year ended, Abel prepared a book-length treatise on elliptic functions titled *Précis d'une théorie des fonctions elliptiques* (Summary of a theory of elliptic functions) that was not published until after his death.

Establishing Rigor in Mathematical Analysis

One of Abel's overriding concerns throughout his entire mathematical career was his desire to make mathematical analysis more rigorous. In all his mathematical writings he paid careful attention to the exactness of his wording and the thoroughness of his proofs. As a student at the Cathedral School, reading the works of Europe's leading mathematicians, he had noticed deficiencies in the logical structure of their arguments. Although 150 years had passed since the invention of calculus, the concepts of derivative and integral were not yet firmly based on a precise definition of limit. He realized that mathematical analysis in the early 19th century lacked the meticulous logic and precision that had characterized classic geometry.

Abel noticed this lack of rigor most prominently in arguments involving infinite series. In an 1826 letter to Holmboe he lamented that, except for the simplest cases, there were no infinite series whose sums had been stringently determined. In the same letter he wrote that he was horrified to hear mathematicians claim that $1^n - 2^n + 3^n - 4^n + \ldots = 1$ for every positive integer n. In his paper on the binomial theorem that appeared later that year, he criticized Cauchy for claiming that an infinite sum of continuous functions would produce a continuous function. As a counterexample he presented the power series of sine functions $\sin(x) - \frac{1}{2}\sin(2x) + \frac{1}{3}\sin(3x) - \frac{1}{4}\sin(4x) + \ldots$ that was discontinuous at every odd multiple of π.

To address the lack of rigor mathematicians used when dealing with infinite series, Abel produced a lengthy two-part paper

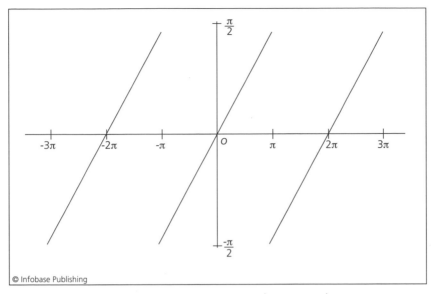

© Infobase Publishing

Abel used the example of the series $y = \sin(x) - \frac{1}{2}\sin(2x) + \frac{1}{3}\sin(3x) - \frac{1}{4}\sin(4x) + \ldots$ to prove that an infinite sum of continuous functions does not always produce a continuous result.

on power series titled "Aufgaben und Lehrsatze" (Problems and theorems) that appeared in *Crelle's Journal* in 1827 and 1828. In this paper he presented new methods for determining the limit of a series, discussed divergent series, and introduced the concept of radius of convergence—the range of values for which an infinite series was equivalent to its corresponding function. Among the techniques he introduced in this paper was the powerful principle now known as Abel's convergence theorem. This rule for certain series of the form $a_1b_1 + a_2b_2 + a_3b_3 + a_4b_4 + \ldots$ generalized the well-known alternating series test that guaranteed that series like $1 - \frac{1}{2} + \frac{1}{3} - \frac{1}{4} + \ldots$ and $1 - \frac{1}{\sqrt{2}} + \frac{1}{\sqrt{3}} - \frac{1}{\sqrt{4}} + \ldots$ converged to finite totals. He also provided summability methods to understand series that are not convergent. Abel, along with Cauchy, Gauss, and German mathematician Karl Weierstrass led the 19th-century effort to make mathematical definitions more precise and mathematical analysis more rigorous.

Death and Legacy

While visiting his fiancée in Froland for Christmas, Abel became so ill that he was confined to bed. He died on April 6, 1829, from complications of tuberculosis. Two days later, Crelle wrote to inform Abel that he had secured an appointment for him at the newly established *Académie Royale des Sciences et des Belles-Lettres de Berlin* (Royal Academy of Sciences and Beautiful Letters in Berlin).

In June 1830 the Paris Academy awarded its *grand prix* (grand prize) to Abel and Jacobi for their outstanding research on elliptic functions. At Jacobi's urging, Cauchy found the memoir on elliptic functions that Abel had submitted to the academy four years earlier. The academy eventually published it in 1841 in their journal *Mémoires présentés par divers savants à l'Académie des Sciences de l'institute national de France* (Reports presented by various scholars to the Academy of Sciences of the National Institute of France). Legendre, upon realizing the significance of the work he had earlier dismissed as illegible, described the treatise as a monument more lasting than bronze. When French mathematician Charles Hermite read the memoir, he predicted that Abel's ideas would keep mathematicians occupied for 500 years.

In 2002 the government of Norway honored the memory of their country's greatest mathematician by instituting the Abel Prize, an award of $750,000 that is given annually to a mathematician in recognition of a lifetime of contributions to the discipline. The award brought to mathematics the same international recognition that the Nobel Prize gave to literature, medicine, and the sciences.

As a tribute to the influence of Abel's ideas, his name is associated with a large number of concepts in several branches of mathematics. Abelian varieties, Abelian integrals, Abelian functions, and Abel's theorem are the central ideas in the theory of elliptic functions. The analysis of infinite series relies on Abel's convergence theorem, Abel's inequality, and Abelian summability. The most widely used idea named after him is the Abelian group—a mathematical structure whose objects satisfy the fundamental property that $a \cdot b = b \cdot a$.

Conclusion

As the prize named in his honor signifies, during Abel's brief lifetime he made significant contributions to the discipline of mathematics. His proof of the impossibility of algebraic formulas to solve equations of degree higher than four not only settled a long-standing question; it also introduced the concept of algebraic field extensions that contributed to the development of abstract algebra. Abel's proof of the general binomial theorem for real and complex powers along with the methods he introduced to analyze the convergence of infinite series helped to establish a rigorous foundation for mathematical analysis. The concepts of elliptic functions and more general classes of doubly periodic functions that he introduced continue to yield new discoveries in the areas of algebra, number theory, and functional analysis.

FURTHER READING

Bell, Eric T. "Genius and Poverty." In *Men of Mathematics*, 307–326. New York: Simon & Schuster, 1965. Chapter 17 presents a biography and evaluation of his mathematical work.

James, Ioan. "Niels Abel (1802–1829)." In *Remarkable Mathematicians from Euler to von Neumann*, 91–97. Washington, D.C.: Mathematical Association of America, 2003. Brief biography and description of his mathematics.

O'Connor, J. J., and E. F. Robertson. "Niels Henrik Abel." In "MacTutor History of Mathematics Archive." University of Saint Andrews. Available online. URL: http://www-groups.dcs.st-andrews.ac.uk/~history/Mathematicians/Abel.html. Accessed on March 17, 2003. Online biography, from the University of Saint Andrews, Scotland.

Ore, Oystein. "Abel, Niels Henrik." In *Dictionary of Scientific Biography*, vol. 1, edited by Charles C. Gillispie, 12–17. New York: Scribner, 1972. Encyclopedic biography, including a detailed description of his mathematical writings.

———. *Niels Henrik Abel: Mathematician Extraordinary*. Minneapolis: University of Minnesota Press, 1957. Authoritative full-length biography.

Stillwell, John. "Elliptic Functions." In *Mathematics and Its History*, 152–166. New York: Springer-Verlag, 1989. Chapter 11 of this college textbook presents a discussion of Abel's most significant discovery and a brief biographical sketch.

Stubhuag, Arild. *Niels Henrik Abel and His Times: Called Too Soon by Flames Afar.* Berlin, Ger: Springer, 2000. Full-length biography translated from the Norwegian by Richard H. Daly with an appendix listing all of Abel's publications.

5

Évariste Galois

(1811–1832)

Évariste Galois formalized the notion of a group, specified a complete set of conditions that determined whether or not an equation was solvable by radicals, and developed the theory of algebraic field extensions now known as Galois theory.
(Granger)

Revolutionary Founder of Group Theory

Évariste Galois (pronounced ay-vah-REEST GAL-wah) died in a duel at the age of 20 after publishing only five short papers detailing his research, but his work had a significant impact on the development of abstract algebra. By formalizing the notion of a group, he laid the foundations of group theory. He developed a theory of solvability of algebraic equations by <u>radicals</u> that grew into the advanced area of algebra known as Galois theory. Better known during his lifetime as a political revolutionary than as a mathematician, Galois's genius was not recognized until many years after he died when mathematicians carefully studied the less than 100 pages of written work that he produced.

Search for the Quintic Formula

Évariste Galois was born on October 25, 1811, in Bourg-la-Reine, France, a small town south of Paris. His father, Nicholas-Gabriel Galois, directed a small boarding school and served as mayor of the town for 14 years. His mother, Adélaïde-Marie Demante Galois, was a well-educated woman who tutored Évariste, his older sister, Nathalie-Théodore, and his younger brother, Alfred, at home until they were in their early teens.

In October 1823 Galois enrolled in Lycée Louis-le-Grand (Louis the Great High School), a well-known high school in Paris named after King Louis XIV. Living conditions at the school were harsh, and the students frequently demonstrated their dissatisfaction with their treatment. In Galois's first year the director expelled 40 students when they sang "Le Marseillaise," the anthem of the French Revolution, rather than raise their glasses in a toast to the king. Initially, Galois earned good grades, winning prizes for excellence in several courses, but he became increasingly discontented with the school's faculty and with his courses in Latin, Greek, and classical literature. By 1827 his academic performance had become so poor that he had to repeat most of his classes.

During this year Galois developed a strong interest in mathematics while taking a course in geometry with H. J. Vernier. Although the class textbook *Géométrie* (Geometry) by French mathematician Adrien-Marie Legendre was intended for a two-year course, Galois read through the book in a matter of days. The book's logical development of geometrical principles fascinated him and stimulated a passionate interest in mathematics. In the school's library he read additional books on algebra and analysis by other leading French mathematicians Augustin-Louis Cauchy and Joseph-Louis Lagrange. Working independently, he successfully mastered the material in these advanced books written for university students, professors, and mathematicians.

As he studied algebra, Galois became intrigued by the formulas that mathematicians used to solve different types of equations. Every linear equation of the form $ax + b = 0$ could be solved using the simple formula $x = -\dfrac{b}{a}$. The quadratic formula $x = \dfrac{-b \pm \sqrt{b^2 - 4ac}}{2a}$ could be used to solve any second-degree equation of the form $ax^2 + bx + c = 0$. Mathematicians had also discovered formulas to solve third- and fourth-degree equations whose highest powered terms were x^3 or x^4, but no one had discovered formulas that worked for higher degree equations.

The task of finding a formula involving square roots and higher roots that would solve all algebraic equations of degree five using finitely many steps attracted Galois's interest. He did not know that such a "quintic formula" had eluded mathematicians for three centuries. After several months of work the 16-year-old student thought he had produced the required formula. His further investigations

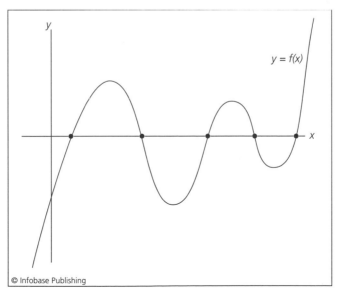

© Infobase Publishing

In his first mathematical research Galois attempted to find a quintic formula to express algebraically all the roots of a polynomial of degree five.

revealed that his formula worked for a limited number of cases but would not solve all fifth-degree equations. After many revisions he became convinced that there was no quintic formula and devoted his efforts to proving this assertion.

Disappointments and Frustrations

At the end of his fifth year of high school Galois took the entrance exam for École Polytechnique (Polytechnic University), a university in Paris established in 1794 by mathematicians Gaspard Monge and Lazare Carnot to provide training in mathematics, science, and engineering for the most talented young men in France. The test focused on material from standard high school mathematics courses that he had not yet taken. As a result of these deficiencies in his knowledge of basic mathematics, he failed the exam and spent a sixth year at Louis-le-Grand.

Vernier, his teacher for his first two mathematics courses, did not appreciate Galois's talents. He criticized Galois for not systematically writing down all the steps in his solutions even though he was able to do many calculations in his head. Louis-Paul-Émile Richard, his math teacher during his final year of high school, recognized his abilities, praised his ingenious methods of solution, and supported his independent research. With Richard's encouragement, Galois wrote a paper titled "Démonstration d'un théorème sur les fractions continues périodiques" (Demonstration of a theorem on continued periodic fractions) that was published in April 1829 in the journal *Annales de mathématiques pures et appliquées* (Annals of pure and applied mathematics). In this short paper he extended a result Lagrange had obtained about continued fractions and gave a more detailed presentation of the concept. This piece of original research by a 17-year-old student demonstrated that he had progressed far beyond his high school courses. Richard was so impressed with this and other evidence of Galois's talents that he suggested that the brilliant young man be admitted to École Polytechnique without having to take the entrance exam.

Galois expanded his work on fifth-degree equations to attempt to find conditions under which formulas existed to solve equations of any degree higher than four. In May and June 1829 he sent to the French Academy of Sciences two papers presenting his research on the solvability of algebraic equations whose degree was a prime number. The secretary of the academy gave the papers to Cauchy, who was impressed with the work but did not communicate his opinions to Galois until the following year.

Two other emotional events in Galois's life added to his frustrations and his feeling of despair. In July his father, humiliated by rumors that his political enemies circulated, committed suicide. At his funeral Galois accused the town's priest of starting the rumors that led to his father's death, and the mourners chased the priest out of the cemetery. In August Galois took the entrance exam for École Polytechnique a second time. When the professor administering the exam insisted that he show his work to justify each step in his solutions, he angrily threw an eraser at him and, consequently, failed the exam.

After six years at Louis-le-Grand, Galois graduated from high school and in November 1829 enrolled as a student at Paris's École Normale (Normal University), a university established to train high school teachers. He was not popular with his instructors or with his fellow students. During one mathematics class the professor announced a new theorem in algebra that had recently been proven but had not yet been published. To embarrass Galois, the professor asked him to go to the board and prove the theorem. When Galois succeeded, the professor criticized his attitude of excessive pride. His only friend, a student named Auguste Chevalier, encouraged Galois to overcome his bitterness and to continue to work on his own mathematical research.

In January 1830 Cauchy was scheduled to present an oral report on Galois's two research papers at a meeting of the academy. Due to an illness he did not give the presentation and never filed a formal report on the work. He privately communicated his positive assessment to Galois, calling to his attention the related results that Norwegian mathematician Niels Henrik Abel had recently obtained. He encouraged Galois to resubmit a single revised paper for the academy's mathematics competition on the topic of solvability of equations. Galois read Abel's research papers, including his 1824 pamphlet in which he proved that there was no quintic formula. Combining Abel's work with his own ideas, he developed a more complete theory on the solvability of higher degree equations by radicals. In February 1830 he sent his new treatise to the academy. Jean-Baptiste Joseph Fourier, the academy's secretary, received the paper but died three months later without having reviewed it. Galois's work was never considered for the *grand prix* (grand prize) that the academy awarded jointly to Abel and German mathematician Carl Gustav Jacobi.

Published Works

Galois had better success with two French mathematics journals that published four of his papers. In April 1830 the *Bulletin des sciences mathématiques* (Bulletin of the mathematical sciences) published an abbreviated summary of the paper he had sent to Fourier at the academy. In this brief article titled "Analyse d'un mémoire sur la résolution algébrique des équations" (Analysis of a memoir on the algebraic resolution of equations), he gave three conditions for the solvability of an irreducible equation whose degree was a prime number. He concisely stated his results and mentioned that he had derived them from Carl Friedrich Gauss's work on the cyclotomic equation $ax^p + b = 0$ and from Cauchy's theory of permutations. Since he did not explain his techniques and did not supply his proofs, few mathematicians understood his work, and none of them recognized the significance of his results.

In June 1830 the *Bulletin des sciences mathématiques* published a second paper, "Note sur la resolution des equations numériques" (Note on the resolution of numerical equations). This paper presented additional results on the use of radicals to solve equations and demonstrated that he had made significant progress beyond Abel's published results but fell short of giving a complete theory on the topic.

His third paper, "Sur la théorie des nombres" (On the theory of numbers), also appeared in the *Bulletin des sciences mathématiques* in June 1830. In this important paper he introduced a new class of numbers that have come to be called "Galois imaginaries." He showed how to construct a mathematical structure known as a finite field of prime order and explained how it was related to the roots of the equation being solved.

In December 1830 the journal *Annales de mathématiques pures et appliqués* published his paper "Notes sur quelques points d'analyse" (Notes on several points of analysis). This short note presenting a few results in analysis was the last mathematical publication during his lifetime.

Political Revolutionary

Despite the successful progress of his mathematical research and the publication of some of his work, Galois grew bitter, resentful, and restless. He joined the Republicans, a group of political revolutionaries who wanted to overthrow the king and set up a new government. In July 1830, when the Republicans started a revolution, Galois made speeches trying to convince his classmates to participate in the rebellion. Mr. Guigniault, the university's director and a strong supporter of the king, locked the doors and gates of the university so the students could not join the uprising. After the successful revolution, Galois wrote a letter to a newspaper explaining how the director had wanted the rebellion to fail but now claimed to be a supporter of the new government. When his "Lettre sur l'enseignement des sciences" (Letter on the teaching of the sciences) appeared in the *Gazette des écoles* (Gazette of the schools), Guigniault expelled him from the university.

Galois joined the Artillery of the National Guard, a branch of the militia primarily composed of Republican revolutionaries. In December 1830 he and his fellow soldiers occupied the royal palace at the Louvre and prepared to stage a revolt against the king. The brief uprising subsided without any violence, the Guard was disbanded, and the wearing of their uniforms was outlawed.

In January 1831 Galois presented a series of public lectures explaining the mathematics he had discovered. He lectured on the theory of Galois imaginaries, algebraic number theory, elliptic functions, and the solvability of equations by radicals. Although 40 students attended his first lecture, fewer students came the second week, only a handful the third week, and not even Galois showed up the fourth week.

For the third time he organized the results of his research on solving algebraic equations and sent it to the Academy of Sciences. This

"Mémoire sur la résolution des équations algébriques" (Memoir on the resolution of algebraic equations) was his most important written work. In this masterpiece he overcame the difficulties that existed in his earlier papers. Combining his own ideas with concepts that had been introduced by Abel, Cauchy, Gauss, Lagrange, and Jacobi, he presented the definitive solution to the problem of the solvability of algebraic equations by radicals. In this memoir and the three papers published in the *Bulletin des sciences mathématiques* he formalized the notion of the algebraic structure known as a group and laid the foundations of group theory, the fundamental component of abstract algebra. These four works also constitute the establishment of the advanced area of abstract algebra now known as Galois theory, in which techniques involving chains of normal subgroups and solvable groups are used to determine when equations are solvable by radicals.

Prison

Galois's passion for political activism continued to match his dedication to mathematics. In May 1831, 19 Republican revolutionaries who had been arrested for conspiracy were found to be innocent. At a banquet to celebrate the court's decision, Galois offered a toast to the death of King Louis-Philippe while holding a glass of wine in one hand and a knife in the other. He was arrested for threatening to kill the king, but was acquitted of the charge. In July 1831 he was arrested again for wearing the uniform of the National Guard and spent the next nine months in Sainte-Pélage prison.

During his prison sentence Galois's life continued to be tumultuous as he attempted to commit suicide and was involved in an uprising by the inmates. In October 1831 he received a letter from the academy rejecting his latest paper. Siméon-Denis Poisson, who reviewed his manuscript, had found his explanations unclear, his proofs difficult to understand, and his theories insufficiently developed. He recommended that Galois resubmit a more complete and detailed presentation of his theory. Galois started to compose the comprehensive manuscript Poisson had suggested, but stopped after writing a five-page preface in which he expressed his anger at the incompetence of the members of the academy to whom he had unsuccessfully submitted his work three times.

Near the end of his prison term, an epidemic of cholera spread through Paris. Fearing a revolt if their political prisoner died in jail, the government authorities transferred Galois to Sieur Faultrier, a hospital facility outside the city, where he served the final six weeks of his sentence. There he fell in love with Stéphanie-Félice du Motel, the daughter of one of the hospital's doctors, and looked forward to starting a new life with her.

The Duel

On April 29, 1832, Galois was released from prison. When his relationship with du Motel ended two weeks later, he was heartbroken and depressed. On May 29 Pescheux d'Herbinville, a Republican revolutionary and a friend of du Motel, challenged him to a duel over her honor. They agreed to settle their dispute with pistols at sunrise.

Galois spent the night outlining his five years of mathematical research on the theory of equations and integral functions. He made notes on three of his unpublished papers. In the margin of the memoir that Poisson had rejected he scribbled that he did not have time to make the few corrections needed to complete the proof. He wrote to his friend Chevalier instructing him to deliver these pages and his unpublished papers to Gauss and Jacobi in the hopes that his work would not die with him.

At dawn on May 30, 1832, 20-year-old Évariste Galois met his opponent for their duel. He was shot in the abdomen and died the next day. Three thousand people attended his funeral on June 2. Republicans rallied and rioted in the streets of Paris for several days. Despite this public demonstration of concern, he was buried in a common grave without a stone to mark the spot.

Mathematicians Recognize the Significance of His Work

For 11 years Galois's brother Alfred and his friend Chevalier brought his final notes and his collection of research papers to Gauss, Jacobi, and other mathematicians throughout Europe. French mathematician Joseph Liouville was the first to recognize the significance of Galois's work. After studying Galois's unique terms and notations and inserting the steps that were missing from his concise proofs, Liouville was able to realize that the results were correct, complete, and important. In September 1843 he presented to the members of the academy a description of Galois's research on solving algebraic equations by radicals.

In October 1846 Liouville published 67 pages of Galois's papers under the title "Oeuvres mathématiques d'Évariste Galois" (Mathematical works of Évariste Galois) in the *Journal de mathématiques pures et appliqués* (Journal of pure and applied mathematics), which he edited. This collection included Galois's five published mathematical papers, the "Lettre à Auguste Chevalier" (Letter to Auguste Chevalier), which he had written the night before the duel, and two unpublished works, "Mémoire sur les conditions de résolubilité des équations par radicaux" (Memoir on the conditions of the resolvability of equations by radicals) and "Des équations primitives qui sont solubles par radicaux" (Primitive equations that are solvable by radicals).

Liouville's amplification of Galois's research and the publication of some of his papers made his work more accessible, but for 20 years few members of the mathematical community understood it. Enrico Betti, Leopold Knonecker, Charles Hermite, and others wrote commentaries on his work and published some results that were immediate applications of it. The third edition of Alfred Serret's *Cours d'algèbre supérieure* (Course in higher algebra) published in 1866 and Camille Jordan's *Traité des substitutions* (Treatise on substitutions) published in 1870 finally integrated group theory and the whole of Galois's work into the main body of mathematics. These two books enabled mathematicians to fully develop his theories and to apply them to a variety of scientific applications. By the end of the 19th century, their explanations and commentaries on Galois's work filled nearly a thousand pages.

In 1906 and 1907 Jules Tannery, the editor of *Bulletin des sciences mathématiques*, published "Manuscrits et papiers inédits de Galois" (Manuscripts and unedited papers of Galois) the complete collection of Galois's research, including 15 additional unpublished papers. In two of these papers, titled "Comment la théorie des équations dépend de celle des permutations" (How the theory of equations depends on that of permutations) and "Recherches sur la théorie des permutations et des équations algébriques" (Research on the theory of permutations and algebraic equations), Galois showed how his work built on Cauchy's results with permutation groups. "Mémoire sur la division des functions elliptiques de première espèce" (Memoir on the division of elliptic functions of the first kind) was a lost manuscript on elliptic functions and Abelian integrals in which he classified those integrals into three categories, an advanced result that Bernhard Riemann independently proved in 1857. The philosophical paper "Discussions sur les progrès de l'analyse pure" (Discussions on the progress of pure analysis) offered a vision for the future of research in algebra, his thoughts about the spirit of modern mathematics, and some reflections on the condition of scientific creativity.

Conclusion

Today mathematicians consider Galois's work on solving algebraic equations by radicals to be a very significant contribution to mathematics. Although Abel had already completely answered the question of solvability of equations, Galois's new techniques extended beyond the immediate problem and introduced a new area of mathematics. His ideas are recognized as the foundation of group theory—the basic component of the study of abstract mathematical structures—and of Galois theory—an advanced area within this branch of mathematics that explains the relationships between solutions of equations and properties of groups.

FURTHER READING

Bell, Eric T. "Genius and Stupidity." In *Men of Mathematics*, 362–377. New York: Simon & Schuster, 1965. Chapter 20 presents an opinionated biography and evaluation of his mathematical work.

Carpenter, Jill. "Évariste Galois 1811–1832 French Algebraist and Group Theorist." In *Notable Mathematicians from Ancient Times to the Present*, edited by Robin V. Young, 193–195. Detroit, Mich.: Gale, 1998. Brief but informative profile of Galois and his work.

Infeld, Leopold. *Whom the Gods Love: The Story of Évariste Galois.* Reston, Va.: National Council of Teachers of Mathematics, 1978. Reprint of the 1948 book-length biography with additional material.

James, Ioan. "Evariste Galois (1811–1832)." In *Remarkable Mathematicians from Euler to von Neumann,* 134–141. Washington, D.C.: Mathematical Association of America, 2003. Brief biography and description of his mathematics.

O'Connor, J. J., and E. F. Robertson. "Evariste Galois." In "MacTutor History of Mathematics Archive." University of Saint Andrews. Available online. URL: http://www-groups. dcs.st-andrews.ac.uk/~history/Mathematicians/Galois.html. Accessed on July 5, 2003. Online biography, from the University of Saint Andrews, Scotland.

Reimer, Luetta, and Wilbert Reimer. "'Don't Let My Life Be Wasted!': Evariste Galois" In *Mathematicians Are People, Too, Stories from the Lives of Great Mathematicians,* 106–113. Parsippany, N.J.: Seymour, 1990. Life story with historical facts and fictionalized dialogue, intended for elementary school students.

Rothman, Tony. "Genius and Biographers: The Fictionalization of Evariste Galois." *American Mathematical Monthly* 89 (1982): 84–106. Scholarly article from mathematics journal that corrects many myths about Galois's life by reference to original correspondence.

Taton, René. "Galois, Evariste." In *Dictionary of Scientific Biography,* vol. 5, edited by Charles C. Gillispie, 259–265. New York: Scribner, 1972. Encyclopedic biography, including a detailed description of his mathematical writings.

Toti Rigatelli, Laura. *Evariste Galois (1811–1832).* Basel: Birkhauser Verlag, 1996. Book-length biography translated from the Italian by John Denton.

Augusta Ada Lovelace

6

(1815–1852)

Augusta Ada Lovelace explained the process of computer programming for Charles Babbage's Analytic Engine. *(The Image Works)*

First Computer Programmer

Augusta Ada Lovelace was the first person to detail the process now known as computer programming. Her extensive notes explaining how to control Charles Babbage's Analytical Engine included a thorough explanation of the steps necessary for calculating the Bernoulli numbers. Her knowledge of mathematics provided her with the understanding necessary to accomplish this historical achievement.

Early Life and Education

Augusta Ada Byron King, countess of Lovelace, was named Augusta Ada Byron when she was born in London, England, on December 10, 1815. Her parents George Gordon Byron and Anne Isabelle Milbanke, Lord and Lady Byron, were wealthy members of England's gentried class. Lord Byron, a passionate and temperamental man and one of England's best-known poets, legally separated from his wife and left the country four months after their daughter's birth. Although he occasionally threatened to take Ada from her mother to be raised by his sister Augusta, he never saw her again, dying in 1824 when she was eight years old.

Lady Byron, who had been called by her poet-husband "the Princess of Parallelograms," shared with her daughter a strong interest in mathematics. Although societal customs prescribed limited exposure to mathematics for upper-class young ladies, Ada's mother encouraged her to learn as much as she could about the subject. In addition to studying mathematics, Ada played the violin and learned to read and speak several languages. She enjoyed making models of boats and once designed plans for a steam-powered airplane.

A series of private tutors directed Ada's education during her childhood and into her adult life. These included William Frend, who had been Lady Byron's mathematics tutor; Mary Somerville, who developed an international reputation as a mathematics and science writer; and Augustus DeMorgan, who later became a professor of mathematics at University College in London.

Ada also participated in the social life of London's upper class, attending the theater, formal balls, concerts, and teas. On May 10, 1833, she was one of the debutantes presented to King William IV and Queen Adelaide at St. James's Palace. At a party in June of that year she met Charles Babbage, the English mathematician who was building a computing device known as the Difference Engine. When she and her mother visited Babbage's London studio two weeks later to view his machine, Ada expressed an interest in the mathematical nature of the machine's design and initiated a lifelong friendship with the inventor.

On July 8, 1835, 19-year-old Ada Byron married William King, a 29-year-old scientist to whom Somerville had introduced her a year earlier. When he was elevated to the status of the first earl of Lovelace in 1838, she became the countess of Lovelace. Although her formal title was Lady Augusta Ada Byron King, countess of Lovelace, she referred to herself as Ada Lovelace. In the first four years of their marriage the couple had three children, whom they named Byron, Annabella, and Ralph. With two houses in the country and one in London, they enjoyed the life of the upper-class gentry. In 1840 her husband, was elected a Fellow of the Royal Society of London, a connection that provided her access to research papers and advanced books that enabled her to continue her mathematical studies.

Babbage's Difference Engine and Analytical Engine

In 1842 Lovelace accepted an opportunity to work with Babbage and write about the computing machines he was designing. She had been corresponding with him since the time of her first visit to his studio to see his Difference Engine in 1833 and had established a friendship with him. In 1834 she had attended a series of lectures on the Difference Engine given by popular science writer Dr. Dionysius Lardner at the Mechanics' Institute and had examined the plans for Babbage's second computing machine, the Analytical Engine. During the early years of her correspondence with Babbage, she discussed their social plans and sought his recommendation of a suitable mathematics tutor. As the years passed, she grew increasingly interested in his mechanical inventions and became knowledgeable about the mathematical principles underlying their design and operation.

Babbage, who had helped to establish Cambridge University's Analytical Society to reform the teaching of mathematics in England and who had been the institution's Lucasian professor of mathematics from 1827 to 1839, had been designing and building computing machines for 20 years. Around 1821 he had begun to consider the construction of a machine that would be capable of making the calculations required to produce mathematical, navigational, and astronomical tables. By 1822 he had built a hand-cranked machine that could calculate and print six-digit tables of logarithmic and astronomical values. He demonstrated the machine for the Royal Society of London and proposed the construction of a more powerful machine capable of making calculations with larger numbers. In 1823 the government agreed to fund his project for three years. He succeeded in building several working models

Lovelace studied the workings of the Analytical Engine—a steam-powered, programmable computing machine that Charles Babbage designed from 1830 to 1870 but never completely built. The machine would have possessed many features of 20th-century electronic computers, including instructions fed in on punched cards, the ability to implement logical branching and condition-controlled looping, and reusable memory locations for variable data. This photo shows two experimental models of portions of the Analytical Engine. (*The Image Works*)

that implemented portions of the machine's functions but never finished the full Difference Engine. In 1842, after the government had invested £17,000 (an amount worth approximately $4 million today) and Babbage had spent £6,000 of his own funds, Prime Minister Sir Robert Peel officially withdrew support for what had been the largest government-sponsored project of its day.

Eight years before this formal announcement, Babbage had already abandoned further development of the Difference Engine and had turned his attention to the design and construction of a more advanced steam-powered, programmable computing machine known as the Analytical Engine. By 1838 he had developed a basic design of a machine whose features included a "store" where intermediate and final numerical results were kept, a "mill" where arithmetic computations were performed, and a set of punched cards that determined the sequence of operations to be performed by the machine. In the process of developing the machine, he produced 300 sheets of engineering drawings and thousands of pages of detailed notes. He never built a working model of his computer partly because contemporary engineering techniques were not sufficiently precise to manufacture the required machine parts.

Lovelace's Writings on the Analytical Engine

In 1840 Babbage delivered a series of seminars to a group of scientists in Turin, Italy, where he explained the workings of his Analytical Engine. Luigi Federico Menabrea, an Italian engineer, ambassador to France, and eventually prime minister of Italy, attended these seminars and agreed to write a journal article about the machine. In October 1842 his paper titled "Notions sur la machine analytique de Charles Babbage" (Ideas on the Analytic Engine of Charles Babbage) appeared in print in the *Bibliothéque Universelle de Genève* (Universal Library of Geneva). Lovelace decided to translate it from French into English so that the description of Babbage's work could be circulated among scientists throughout England. Early in 1843 through the intercession of Charles Wheatstone, a scientist, inventor, professor, and family friend, she contracted with Richard

Taylor to include her work in his *Scientific Memoirs*, a collection of translations of scientific articles from the transactions of foreign academies of science that he published from 1837 to 1852. Babbage agreed to assist her in the six-month project, and her husband supported her work by copying drafts of her manuscript.

As Lovelace translated Menabrea's paper into English, she identified several topics that required more detailed explanations. When she rejected Babbage's suggestion that she write an original paper on the subject, he recommended that she include some original supplementary material in a set of notes appended to the memoir. After generating numerous drafts and revisions that Babbage critiqued, she produced seven notes comprising 40 pages, more than twice as long as Menabrea's 17-page paper. The finished work appeared in the August 1843 edition of *Scientific Memoirs* under the title " 'Sketch of the Analytical Engine Invented by Charles Babbage' by L. F. Menabrea of Turin, Officer of the Military Engineers, au *Bibliothéque Universelle de Genève*, nouvelle serie, xli, October, 1842, no. 82; with Notes upon the Memoir by the Translator, A. A. L." ('Sketch of the Analytical Engine Invented by Charles Babbage' by L. F. Menabrea of Turin, Officer of the Military Engineers, from the Universal Library of Geneva, New Series, xli, October, 1842, no. 82; with Notes upon the Memoir by the Translator, A. A. L.)." Lovelace's name did not appear as the translator although her initials A. A. L. appeared at the end of each note.

In his paper Menabrea described the nature and extent of the capabilities of Babbage's Difference Engine and extolled the extended functionality that the Analytical Engine would provide. He explained that when the Analytical Engine was built it would perform the four arithmetical operations of addition, subtraction, multiplication, and division directly through the mechanical interaction of a series of gears. In addition to making rapid and accurate computations, it would also be capable of implementing logical analysis to modify its sequence of operations when it detected that specified conditions had been met. This facility would enable the machine to use counters and conditions to control looping and branching operations so that once it had been set to work on a problem it would require no further intervention from the operator. He mentioned the machine's ability to create a library of tables in which it would store collections of logarithms and other commonly used values, and he reiterated Babbage's claim that his machine would be able to multiply two 20-digit numbers in three minutes.

In her eight-page "Note A," Lovelace explained the fundamental distinctions between Babbage's earlier Difference Engine and his more advanced Analytical Engine. She explained that the older device was capable of evaluating any polynomial of degree six or less using the method of finite differences and printing a table of results. This method reduced the process of computation of each function value to a series of at most six additions, the only arithmetic operation that the machine actually performed. While being careful not to disparage the power of the Difference Engine for producing accurate tables of numerical values, she contrasted its

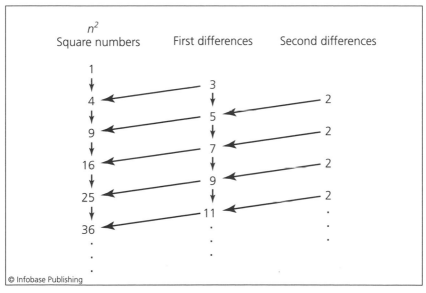

Babbage's Difference Engine used the method of finite differences to generate tables of values for polynomials of degree at most six. This chart, similar to one in Lovelace's translation of Menabrea's paper, illustrates how the machine calculated successive values of the polynomial n^2. After the operator supplied the initial value in each column, each subsequent value in the first two columns was calculated as the sum of the two entries directly above it and to its right.

limited functionality with that of the Analytical Engine, which could perform four operations—addition, subtraction, multiplication, and division—in the process of manipulating more complex expressions. The newer machine could solve systems of linear equations, multiply polynomials, evaluate an unlimited portion of an infinite series, and perform symbolic as well as arithmetic manipulations. She explained that the Analytical Engine's versatility was provided by a set of punched cards in which different patterns of holes corresponded to different mathematical symbols. These cards were similar to those used to control the Jacquard loom that could weave intricate patterns in textiles. The selection and sequencing of these control cards determined which operations the machine performed and in what order they were executed. In a forward-looking prediction of computer-generated music, she suggested that the machine would be capable of creating elaborate musical compositions if the characteristics of music could be quantified appropriately.

The five-page "Note B" described the design and operation of the storehouse—the collection of gears that formed the machine's memory. The set of gears and dials stacked together on each axle physically represented the value saved in one variable at the start of the program or during its computational process. Using the values $a = 5$, $x = 98$, and $n = 7$ stored in three variables, Lovelace explained how the Analytical Engine could be made to evaluate the expressions ax^n, x^{an}, $a \cdot n \cdot x$, $\dfrac{a}{n}x$, and $a + x + n$ by supplying it with the proper sequence of control cards. Her explanations distinguished the supplying variables whose values were used during the computation and the receiving variable where the resulting value was then stored. She mentioned in the one-page "Note C" that a block of operations known as a cycle could be performed multiple times by backing up the cards and processing them repeatedly.

In the five-page "Note D" Lovelace methodically explained the sequence of 11 operations (six multiplications, three subtractions, and two divisions) required to perform the evaluation of the expressions $\dfrac{dn' - d'n}{mn' - m'n} = x$ and $\dfrac{d'm - dm'}{mn' - m'n}$. She presented a detailed chart resembling an assembly language computer program that exhibited the incremental changes effected by each of the 11 operations with the 16 supplying and receiving variables. This meticulous chart generalized the similar seven-line chart Menabrea had included to detail the process of calculating the value labeled as x. In her explanation of the sequence of steps she emphasized the machine's ability to save intermediate results (such as the common denominator of the two given expressions) for use in multiple computations. She also provided an explanation of the method used to implement an "increment" operation such as $V_n = V_n + V_p$ in which the same variable played both a supplying and receiving role.

Lovelace was careful to distinguish the analytical abilities of the machine from its capacity for numerical computation. In the nine-page "Note E" she explained how the machine could multiply the two trigonometric expressions $A + A_1 \cos(\theta) + A_2 \cos(2\theta) + A_3 \cos(3\theta) + \ldots$ and $B + B_1 \cos(\theta)$. She showed that the well-known formula $\cos(n\theta) \cdot \cos(\theta) = \frac{1}{2}\cos((n+1)\theta) + \frac{1}{2}\cos((n-1)\theta)$ could be used to enable the machine to determine the coefficients of the resulting series $C + C_1 \cos(\theta) + C_2 \cos(2\theta) + C_3 \cos(3\theta) + \ldots$ without knowing in advance a specific formula for their computation. She emphasized that the algebraic capabilities of the machine extended to manipulations of infinite series for logarithms, sines, tangents, and other nonpolynomial functions.

The brief two-page "Note F" exhibited a process for reducing to upper triangular form a system of 10 linear equations involving 10 variables. Lovelace explained that in the repetitive process of eliminating the first variable from the last nine equations, eliminating the second variable from the last eight equations, and continuing until the tenth equation had only a single variable the 330 operations required could be implemented by reusing a cycle of three cards 110 times. She cited this application as another example of the machine's ability to obtain a mathematical solution without being given a complete formula for doing it. She concluded this note with a prediction that the machine's ability to do long series of involved computations would enable mathematicians to deduce new results that they would not have otherwise considered.

The most historically significant portion of Lovelace's writings was the 10-page "Note G" in which she presented the first computer program. In both verbal and chart form she presented a detailed explanation of the process for calculating a sequence of values known as the Bernoulli numbers. After deriving a recursive formula, Lovelace showed how the machine could determine the Bernoulli number B_{2n} after calculating and storing the smaller values B_0, B_1, B_2, . . . , B_{2n-1}. The program for calculating the Bernoulli numbers was much more logically complicated than the 11-line sequence of instructions detailed in "Note D" where each operation was implemented a single time in the specified order. The order in which the steps of this program were implemented depended on the machine's ability to evaluate quantities and then choose to perform a cycle of steps again or to carry out a different operation. These concepts of looping and branching distinguish a static list of instructions from a logical computer program. The minuscule detail of her explanation of the program includes a computation of the total number of additions, subtractions, multiplications, and divisions required in the process.

"Note G" also included other significant information about the Analytical Engine. The initial section of the note summarized six of the machine's features. In addition to its ability to perform the four arithmetic operations and its capacity for processing an unlimited number of quantities each of unbounded magnitude, Lovelace cited its ability to perform both arithmetic and algebraic analysis. She mentioned the machine's capacity to work with both positive and negative numbers, the opportunity to substitute one formula for another, and the machine's ability to modify its sequence of instructions when it detected a value that was zero or "infinite." She also briefly discussed how the machine could be made to calculate derivatives and integrals for expressions of the form ax^n as well as for power series.

Later Activities

The publication of Lovelace's translation and notes generated high praise from knowledgeable sources. Babbage called her work the best contemporary account of his machine and confidently declared that it would enable scientists to realize that the entire process of analysis was now capable of being executed by machine. Somerville congratulated Lovelace on the clarity with which she had illustrated such a difficult subject. Although the published work acknowledged only her initials "A. A. L.," most people within the small scientific community of London knew that she was the author.

Lovelace had hoped that the success of her translation would propel her to a career as a science writer. In letters to Babbage and Somerville she described her publication on the Analytical Engine as the first of many children that she hoped to create. She made plans to hire tutors and nannies to care for her three actual children, freeing her to pursue her writing career. She proposed to Babbage that he hire her to manage the paperwork, produce the technical documents, and publicize his Analytical Engine for the three years that he estimated it would take to complete the development of the machine. When Babbage declined her offer, she inquired about a position as science adviser to England's Prince Albert and began collecting materials on microscopic analysis of the human nervous and circulatory systems, electrical circuits, poisons, the occult, hypnosis, and the history of several scientific discoveries. She offered to collaborate with scientists Michael Faraday and Andrew Crosse on experiments and writing projects about electricity. Although she considered an array of potential projects and started a lesser number of them, her only published work consisted of a few paragraphs and footnotes that she contributed to a review her husband wrote in 1848 of French agronomist De Gasparin's book on the effects of climate on the growth of crops.

Lovelace spent her final years surrounded by controversy and scandal. Throughout her life she suffered from asthma, digestive problems, intense mood swings, depression, and hallucinations. Seeking scientific treatments to remedy these physical ailments, she experimented with opium, cannabis, morphine, and alcohol. With Babbage she developed a betting scheme based on a flawed theory of mathematical probabilities. She lost so much money wagering on horse races that she had to sell some of her valuable jewelry to pay her gambling debts, and her husband had to intercede with her creditors. Lovelace died on November 27, 1852, from cancer of the uterus.

Conclusion

Although Babbage died without building his Analytical Engine, computer scientists regard him as the "Father of Modern Computing" because he designed the first programmable computer based on the principles of stored instructions that control and modify the machine's behavior. As the writer who set down the first clear exposition of how to communicate with and control such a machine, Lovelace was the first computer programmer. Her 19th-century writings did not directly influence the programmers of 20th-century computers, but they cite her work as the beginning of their profession.

Lovelace's notes on Babbage's machine were rediscovered and published in 1953 in a volume by B. Y. Bowden entitled *Faster Than Thought: A Symposium on Digital Computing Machines.* In 1980 the United States government announced its intention to develop a new standardized programming language called Ada in her honor. All military and governmental applications were to be developed in this language, enabling different groups to use segments of programming code that other groups had developed and facilitating communication between federal computer systems. The Association for Women in Computing, a professional organization in information technology, honors women who make outstanding contributions to the field of computer science through their annual Augusta Ada Lovelace Award.

FURTHER READING

Baum, Joan. *The Calculating Passion of Ada Byron.* Hamden, Conn.: Archon Books, 1986. Book-length biography with emphasis on her published translation and notes.

Henderson, Harry. "Charles Babbage (1792–1871) and Ada Lovelace (1815–1852)." In *Modern Mathematicians,* 1–15. New York: Facts On File, 1996. Brief biographical profile discussing their lives and their joint work on the analytical engine.

Moore, Doris Langley. *Ada, Countess of Lovelace: Byron's Legitimate Daughter.* New York: Harper & Row, 1977. Book-length biography.

O'Connor, J. J., and E. F. Robertson. "Augusta Ada King, countess of Lovelace." In "MacTutor History of Mathematics Archive." University of Saint Andrews. Available online. URL: http:// www-groups.dcs.st-andrews.ac.uk/~history/Mathematicians/ Lovelace.html. Accessed on March 14, 2003. Online biography, from the University of Saint Andrews, Scotland.

Perl, Teri. "Ada Byron Lovelace (1815–1852)." *Math Equals: Biographies of Women Mathematicians + Related Activities*, 100–125. Menlo Park, Calif.: Addison-Wesley, 1978. Biography accompanied by exercises related to her work.

Rappaport, Karen D. "Augusta Ada Lovelace (1815–1852)." In *Women of Mathematics: A Biobibliographic Sourcebook*, edited by Louise S. Grinstein and Paul J. Campbell, 135–139. New York: Greenwood, 1987. Biographical profile with an evaluation of her work in mathematics and computer science accompanied by an extensive list of references.

Reimer, Luetta, and Wilbert Reimer. "Conducting the Computer Symphony: Ada Lovelace." In *Mathematicians Are People, Too, Stories from the Lives of Great Mathematicians, Volume Two*, 100– 107. Parsippany, N.J.: Seymour, 1995. Life story with historical facts and fictionalized dialogue, intended for elementary school students.

Reinherz, Leslie. "Ada Byron, Countess of Lovelace 1815–1852 English Applied Mathematician." In *Notable Mathematicians from Ancient Times to the Present*, edited by Robin V. Young, 85–87. Detroit, Mich.: Gale, 1998. Brief but informative description of her life and work.

Stein, Dorothy. *Ada: A Life and a Legacy*. Cambridge, Mass.: MIT Press, 1985. Book-length biography.

Toole, Betty Alexandra. *Ada, the Enchantress of Numbers*. Mill Valley, Calif.: Strawberry Press, 1992. Book-length biography.

Walker, John. "The Analytical Engine," in "Librorum Liberorum." Fourmilab, Switzerland. Available online. URL: http://www. fourmilab.to/babbage/. Accessed on July 15, 2005. Discussion of Babbage's Analytical Engine, includes the full text of Lovelace's translation and notes.

Wall, Elizabeth S. "Babbage and the Countess." *Electronic Education* (February 1986): 10. Single-page article in education journal highlighting Lovelace's contributions to computing.

Woolley, Benjamin. *The Bride of Science: Romance, Reason, and Byron's Daughter.* New York: McGraw-Hill, 1999. Book-length biography.

Florence Nightingale

7

(1820–1910)

Florence Nightingale used graphical presentations of medical and health statistics to convince governmental leaders to reform conditions in England's hospitals, military barracks, and infirmaries.
(*Granger*)

Health Care Based on Statistics

Florence Nightingale was one of the first public figures to use statistical information as a basis for making positive changes in societal practices. As the supervisor of all British nurses during the Crimean War she documented the reduction in mortality rates that accompanied her introduction of new nursing practices in military hospitals. An avid student of mathematics, she introduced the polar area diagram as a graphical technique for presenting an effective visual summary of categorical data. Her graphical presentations of medical and health statistics convinced governmental and military leaders to implement widespread reforms in England's hospitals, military barracks, and infirmaries. The training program she established for nurses and her books on nursing introduced significant international changes to the nursing profession.

Interests in Nursing and Mathematics

Florence Nightingale was born on May 12, 1820, to William Edward Nightingale and Frances Smith, a wealthy English couple who were vacationing in Florence, Italy. Her father, a rich landowner and high sheriff of the county, had changed his last name from Shore after inheriting an estate in Derbyshire, England, from his great-uncle Peter Nightingale. Her mother was one of 11 children of politician William Smith, who had served in England's parliament for 40 years. Florence and her older sister, Parthenope, were born during a two-year tour of Europe that their parents' took immediately after their wedding. Each daughter was named after the Italian city in which she was born, Parthenope being the Greek name for Naples.

Nightingale's family enjoyed the comforts and the social life of England's upper class. In the 1825 they moved to a new country estate in Derbyshire named Lea Hurst, and in 1826 they purchased a larger house in Hampshire called Embley Park. The children received their early education from a series of nannies and private tutors who taught them reading, writing, English history, Scripture, and arithmetic. As they grew older, their father taught them world history, Greek, Latin, French, German, Italian, and mathematics. At their two spacious homes the Nightingales entertained distinguished foreign visitors and the elite of London's society.

From an early age Nightingale demonstrated a strong interest in nursing, a career deemed inappropriate for a lady of her social standing. In her diaries she recorded the details of her successful effort as a young girl to care for a dog that had broken its paw and her impressions of visits that she made with her mother to the homes of sick neighbors. As she grew older, her relatives and friends sought her assistance and counsel whenever they were ill. During an 18-month family vacation to Europe in 1837–38 she visited a school in Genoa, Italy, for children who could not hear or speak. On other trips abroad she visited hospitals and schools operated by orders of religious sisters in Edinburgh, Scotland; Dublin, Ireland; Paris, France; Rome, Italy; and Alexandria, Egypt. In 1850 and 1851 she made two extended visits to the Deaconess Institute of Kaiserwerth near Düsseldorf, Germany, where she observed in detail the operations of the medical facility and the administration of the religious community of nurses.

In addition to her attraction to nursing, Nightingale developed a strong interest in mathematics. At the age of 20 she convinced her parents to allow her to study higher mathematics rather than needlework and dancing. Her algebra and geometry tutors included James Joseph Sylvester, who later became a mathematics professor at the Royal Military Academy at Woolwich and president of the London Mathematical Society. For a brief period of time Nightingale tutored children and taught arithmetic and geometry at the Ragged School, an educational institution for poor children in London. Her letters to friends indicated that she was familiar with the history of mathematics and episodes from the lives of famous mathematicians.

Nightingale developed a deep interest in the developing area of statistics—the branch of mathematics concerned with the analysis of data. She read Belgian mathematician Adolphe Quetelet's 1835 book *Sur l'homme et le developpement de ses facultés, essai d'une physique sociale* (On man and the development of his faculties, essay of a social physics) in which he introduced the idea that the measurements of any human trait were distributed according to a normal curve around those of the "average man." Nightingale also attended the 1847 meeting of the British Association for the Advancement of Science in Oxford where F. G. P. Neison presented a statistical report showing that the crime rate was lower in counties where people were better educated. She learned that a small number of economists had started to use statistical evidence in their analysis of societal conditions.

In her diary and her published writings from the early 1850s Nightingale wrote about the events that led her to her decision to devote her life to a career in nursing. In 1951 she anonymously published a pamphlet titled *The Institution of Kaiserwerth on the Rhine* in which she described the favorable impressions she had gained during her first visit to that nursing facility. The following year she wrote *Suggestions for Thought to Searchers after Religious Truth among the Artisans of England,* a three-volume manuscript that she privately published in 1860 in which she shared aspects of her personal philosophy, including her opinions that marriage was selfish and that women should seek fulfillment in a career. In 1854 her sister, Parthenope, who was an accomplished novelist, compiled and edited a collection of Nightingale's correspondence from her five-month trip to Egypt under the title *Letters from Egypt, A Journey on the Nile, 1849–1850.* This travelogue, which circulated widely throughout England, included many of her reflections on the state of health care and education as well as the role of women in Egyptian society. In her diary during those months she recorded five visions in which God called her to dedicate her life to his service. Upon returning to England, she ended her nine-year romance with Richard Monckton Milnes, a poet and social reformer who later became Lord Houghton, and committed herself to a career in nursing.

In 1853, at the age of 33, Nightingale accepted an unpaid position as superintendent at the Invalid Gentlewoman's Institution in London. She introduced sweeping changes in nursing procedures, requiring the nurses to sleep in quarters adjacent to the patients' ward and to attend to the patients' needs whenever they rang bells set up for that purpose. She installed mechanical improvements such as piped hot water and elevators to deliver patients' meals to the ward and increased the hospital's capacity to 27 beds. Within three months she replaced the chaplain, the head physician, and almost the entire staff of nurses and housekeepers. Despite these programmatic improvements, she was unable to implement one of her main goals—the institution of a program to train women to become nurses.

Nursing during the Crimean War

In October 1854 Nightingale responded to a governmental initiative to recruit female nurses to serve in military hospitals near the Black Sea, where British, French, and Turkish forces were fighting the Russian army in the Crimean War. Through the intercession of several influential friends, including Sidney Herbert, the secretary at war, she was appointed to the position of superintendent of the Female Nursing Establishment in the English General Military Hospitals in Turkey. In November she and her staff of 38 nurses from Ireland, England, and France arrived in Scutari, a suburb of Constantinople, where they were assigned to Barrack Hospital, the main British medical facility in the Crimean War zone. In addition to the military budget allocated to her office, she controlled a fund of £9,000 that had been raised through private donations in England for her nursing mission.

Although her official responsibilities were to supervise the nurses in four local hospitals, Nightingale regularly exceeded the limits of her authority, introducing broad changes in all aspects of the hospitals' operations. She built new kitchen and laundry facilities, insulated the walls of the hospitals, and introduced new procedures for food preparation and daily housekeeping. With her private funds she bought fruits, vegetables, higher-quality meats, supplies of bandages, and additional medicines. Although it took four months to fully institute these improvements, she immediately implemented a meticulous system of record-keeping that brought order to the hospitals' haphazard operations and allowed her to monitor the effect of the changes she made.

Nightingale's records showed that during November 1854, the month that she had arrived, more than 60 percent of the patients admitted to the Scutari Hospital had died. By February 1855, the last month before her program of improvements was fully implemented, the changes she had made reduced the death rate to 43 percent. In June, after three full months under her new system of nursing and hospital procedures, the death rate had dropped to 2 percent. At French military hospitals where no procedural changes were implemented, the death rate persisted at nearly 40 percent throughout the entire war.

Articles written by war correspondents for *The Times*, London's major newspaper, praised the effectiveness of Nightingale's work and proclaimed her a national heroine. When Queen Victoria was notified by telegram in May 1855 that Nightingale had become ill with typhus, she ordered Lord Raglan, the commander in chief of the British military forces in Crimea, to visit the distinguished patient and convey her best wishes. In October Lord Panmore, the new secretary of war, named her general superintendent of the Female Nursing Establishment of the Military Hospitals of the Army, extending her responsibilities to all British hospitals throughout the entire war zone. The War Office adopted her policies on standardization and monitoring of food, clothing, and furniture as official procedures for all military hospitals. A Royal Warrant implemented her revisions of the duties and pay of medical officers.

Statistical Analysis of Military Mortality Rates

In July 1856, four months after the end of the war, Nightingale returned to England to widespread public acclaim. She used her reputation and visibility to publicize the unsanitary conditions in which British soldiers were forced to live. In meetings with Prime Minister Palmerston, Queen Victoria, and Prince Albert she discussed the need for large-scale reforms in military housing and hospitals. Despite resistance from the War Office, in May 1857 the government established the Royal Commission on the Health of the Army. Although she was not permitted to serve on the committee, Nightingale strongly influenced its work through her friendship with Herbert, who headed the commission and by providing the committee with much of its information.

In 1858 Nightingale submitted to the commission an 800-page report titled *Notes on Matters Affecting the Health, Efficiency, and Hospital Administration of the British Army, Founded Chiefly on the Experience of the Late War*. Her extensive report presented graphical summaries of mortality rates of British soldiers during peacetime

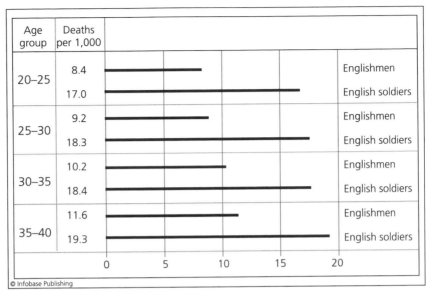

Age group	Deaths per 1,000							
20–25	8.4							Englishmen
	17.0							English soldiers
25–30	9.2							Englishmen
	18.3							English soldiers
30–35	10.2							Englishmen
	18.4							English soldiers
35–40	11.6							Englishmen
	19.3							English soldiers
		0	5	10	15	20		

© Infobase Publishing

Nightingale used line diagrams similar to this graphic to contrast visually the death rates among British soldiers and civilians during peacetime. A comparison of the lengths of each pair of line segments revealed that in each of the four age categories the military death rate per 1,000 men was almost twice as high as the corresponding civilian death rate.

and during the Crimean War. Using line diagrams, she showed that in each of four age categories the nearly 2 percent rate of death among soldiers living in military barracks during peacetime was approximately twice as high as the mortality rate for male civilians. She concluded that for the 55,000-member British Army this meant that forcing healthy soldiers to live in military housing was as criminal as shooting 1,100 soldiers each year. Using area diagrams, she showed that if the army recruited 10,000 20-year-old males per year and each recruit remained in military service until age 40, the military death and "invaliding" rates would reduce the strength of the army from a potential of 200,000 to 142,000. In an accompanying diagram she showed that if the military death and invaliding rates were reduced to the significantly lower civilian rates, the strength of the same army would rise to 167,000 able-bodied soldiers.

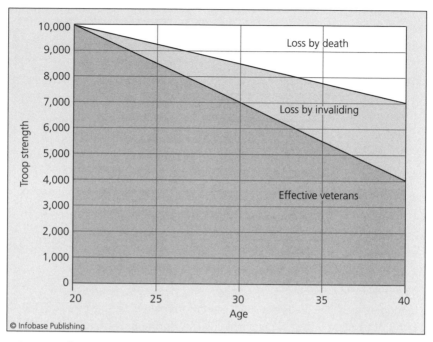

Using area diagrams similar to this one, Nightingale presented visual summaries of the British army's loss of manpower due to deaths and permanent injuries. The areas of the two triangular regions indicated that deaths and injuries depleted the strength of the military forces by 29 percent.

Nightingale's report introduced a new type of graphical summary that came to be called a polar area chart or a "coxcomb" because it resembled the red crest on the top of a rooster's head. She used two diagrams of this type to present a visual summary of the number of deaths in all British military hospitals during the Crimean War from April 1854 to March 1856. For each 12-month period from April to March, she displayed the data in the form of 12 wedges with equal central angles radiating from a common point. The area of each wedge was proportional to the number of deaths in the corresponding month. Within each wedge she grouped the monthly mortality figures into three categories by cause of death: the outer portion that she shaded blue represented deaths due to preventable or contagious diseases such as cholera or typhus; the middle region that she shaded pink represented deaths from wounds; and the inner gray portion represented deaths from all other causes. Her graphical presentation showed that deaths in military hospitals peaked in January 1855, when 3,168 soldier died—2,761 (87 percent) from contagious diseases, 83 (3 percent) from wounds, and 324 (10 percent) from other causes. These deaths represented almost 10 percent of the 32,000-member British Army contingent in Crimea. She remarked that, if these mortality rates had continued, deaths due

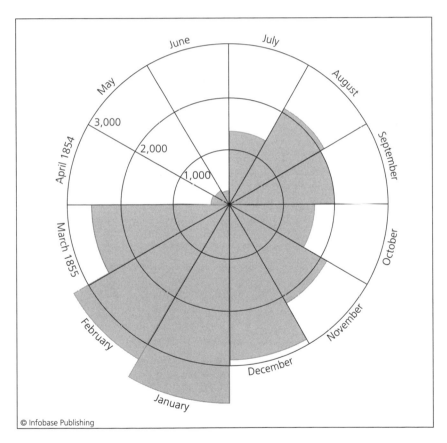

© Infobase Publishing

In her report to the War Office, Nightingale introduced polar area or cox-comb diagrams to summarize graphically how many British soldiers died each month during the Crimean War. Each wedge was subdivided to indicate the number of deaths in a single month due to contagious diseases, war wounds, and other causes.

to contagious diseases alone would have wiped out the entire army in less than a year.

English physician and statistician William Farr described Nightingale's report as the best document ever written on statistical diagrams or on the army. The commission included much of her data in their 1858 report, relegating most of her diagrams to an appendix. Convinced that her graphical presentations of the data would be more effective than the textual report in convincing governmental leaders, military officials, and ordinary citizens of the need for reforms, she privately printed and circulated 2,000 copies of a collection of her tables under the title *Mortality of the British Army, at Home, at Home and Abroad, and during the Russian War, as Compared with the Mortality of the Civil Population in England.* In 1859 she produced a similar pamphlet titled *A Contribution to the Sanitary History of the British Army in the Late War with Russia,* which presented graphical summaries based on revised figures taken from the commission's report.

The attention that these reports and Nightingale's personal efforts focused on military mortality rates moved the government to establish four subcommissions to implement the commission's recommendations. The group responsible for making physical alterations to military hospitals and barracks introduced improvements in kitchens, water supply, sewerage, and ventilation. The other three subcommissions created a sanitary code for the military, established an army medical school, and designed revised procedures for gathering medical statistics. In honor of her pioneering work on this project the Statistical Society of England elected her to its membership in 1858.

International Improvements in Health Care

During the first four years after the Crimean War, Nightingale actively participated in several additional initiatives to improve health care conditions both in her own country and internationally. In 1858 she and Farr designed data forms and mailed them to British military stations throughout India to collect information on the sanitary conditions in which soldiers were living. By 1859 she successfully promoted for the establishment of a Royal Sanitary Commission for India. She submitted her own report to the commission, identifying defective sewerage systems, overcrowded living conditions, lack of exercise, and inferior hospital facilities as the reasons why the death rate among soldiers in India was six times higher than among soldiers in England. The commission's 1863 *Report on the Army in India* included her comments in a section titled "Observations by Miss Nightingale." The implementation of their recommended reforms reduced the annual death rate among soldiers in India from 7 percent to 2 percent during the next 10 years.

Convinced that ineffective hospital policies could be changed by arguments based on statistical evidence, Nightingale and Farr collaborated on the design of a standard form to collect medical data from hospitals throughout the world. Their form requested annual information on the number of patients admitted, discharged, and deceased, the average length of a patient's stay, and the number of patients treated for each of numerous categories of diseases. Although the 1860 International Congress of Statistics approved their Model Hospital Statistical Form, it was never adopted universally due to its complex structure and its controversial categorization of diseases.

In addition to her work with national commissions and international organizations, Nightingale effected changes in health care practices through her books on nursing and hospitals. In 1859 she wrote a manual titled *Notes on Nursing: What It Is and What It Is Not*. The most popular of her 200 published works, the manual sold 15,000 copies in its first month. The book presented a description of the fundamental principles of nursing, emphasizing that, in addition to administering medicine and changing bandages, nursing required attention to the proper use of light, fresh air, warmth, cleanliness, quiet, and healthy diet at the least expense of the patient's energy. Two years later, she published *Notes on Nursing for the Labouring Classes*, an inexpensive, abridged version for the general public that included an additional chapter titled "Minding Baby." In 1859 she also wrote *Notes on Hospitals* in which she enunciated the essential principle that a hospital should do the sick no harm. This book included guidelines for how hospitals should be built and the functional reasons for those guidelines.

One of Nightingale's original motivations for entering the nursing profession had been to establish training programs for nurses. Drawing on the assets of the Nightingale Fund, a collection of private donations that had grown to £50,000, she opened the Nightingale School at St. Thomas Hospital in London on July 9, 1860, with an initial class of 15 student nurses. This first school of modern nursing emphasized rules on deportment, dress, and report writing as well as the elements of nursing described in her 1859 book. The initiative was so successful that seven years later the Metropolitan Poor Act mandated the hiring of trained nurses in all workhouse infirmaries in London. Within 15 years her school responded to requests to send nurses to start similar schools throughout Europe and well as in Australia, Canada, and the United States.

Although Nightingale suffered health problems that confined her to her room for the last 30 years of her life, she continued to correspond with international acquaintances and wrote books and papers on nursing. She served as a consultant on army health during the American Civil War and advised the British War Office about military medical care in Canada. During the Franco-Prussian War of 1870, both France and Prussia sought her advice on setting up field hospitals to treat their wounded. Her further writings on nursing included an 1871 book titled *Introductory Notes on Lying in Institutions,* two articles for *Quain's Dictionary of Medicine* in 1882, and a paper titled "Sick-Nursing and Health-Nursing" for the Chicago Exhibition of 1893. In recognition of her contributions to military nursing the War Office awarded her the Royal Red Cross in 1883 and elected her to membership in the prestigious Order of Merit in 1907. She died in her sleep on August 13, 1910, at her apartment in London. Her family refused the queen's offer to bury her in Westminster Abbey, an honor reserved for the most distinguished citizens of Great Britain.

Conclusion

During the Crimean War Nightingale spent many hours each night walking through hospital wards visiting wounded soldiers. In his 1857 poem "Santa Filomena" (Saint Filomena) American poet Henry Wadsworth Longfellow popularized this image of her as the compassionate lady with the lamp. More important than her personal treatment of individual patients was her work as an administrator, author, consultant, and influential public figure who used statistical reasoning to reform health conditions in hospitals, military barracks, and infirmaries. She introduced the polar area diagram as a graphical technique for presenting an effective visual summary of categorical data. In an era when statistics was still a new branch of mathematics, she effectively demonstrated that statistical information could be used to make positive changes in societal practices.

FURTHER READING

Cohen, Bernard I. "Florence Nightingale." *Scientific American* 250 (1984): 128–137. Magazine article discussing Nightingale's use of statistics to improve hospital mortality rates, with illustrations from her book and commission reports.

Lipsey, Sally. "Mathematical Education in the Life of Florence Nightingale." Newsletter of the Association for Women in Mathematics 23, no. 4 (July/August 1993), 11–12. Brief article discussing Nightingale's work as a mathematics tutor and as a consultant on health care projects.

Nightingale, Florence. *Letters from Egypt, A Journey on the Nile, 1849–1850.* New York: Weidenfeld and Nicolson, 1987. Selected correspondence written by Nightingale to her family during her five-month visit to Egypt.

O'Connor, J. J., and E. F. Robertson. "Florence Nightingale." In "MacTutor History of Mathematics Archive." University of Saint Andrews. Available online. URL: http://www-groups.dcs.st-andrews.ac.uk/~history/Mathematicians/Nightingale.html.

Accessed on March 14, 2003. Online biography, from the University of Saint Andrews, Scotland.

Seymer, Lucy Ridgely. *Florence Nightingale*. London: Faber & Faber, 1950. Book-length biography.

Smith, Francis Barrymore. *Florence Nightingale: Reputation and Power*. New York: St. Martin's Press, 1982. Book-length biography focusing on health care reforms.

8

Georg Cantor

(1845–1918)

Georg Cantor introduced radical ideas about infinite sets that established set theory as a new branch of mathematics.
(Courtesy of the Library of Congress)

Father of Set Theory

Georg Cantor introduced radical ideas about infinite sets that established set theory as a new branch of mathematics. Using diagonal arguments, he established one-to-one correspondences between the natural numbers, the rational numbers, and the algebraic numbers and between the points in a square and the points on a line segment. He proved the existence of different orders of infinity by showing that the real numbers formed an uncountable set and that the power set of any infinite set had a higher cardinality than the set itself. His introduction of the continuum hypothesis, the well-ordering principle, the trichotomy of cardinals, and the set of all sets led mathematicians to the development of a rigorous theory of sets.

Family Life and Education

Georg Ferdinand Ludwig Philipp Cantor was born on March 3, 1845, in St. Petersburg, Russia. Georg Woldemar Cantor, his father, was a prosperous merchant and stockbroker who had moved from Denmark to Russia. Maria Anna Böhm, his mother, came from a family of violinists and music teachers. Although both his parents were of Jewish descent, his Lutheran father and Catholic mother raised him as a devout Christian. The oldest of six children, he learned to read and write from his mother before attending elementary school in St. Petersburg.

When his father became ill in 1856, the family moved to Germany, where the climate was milder, settling in Wiesbaden and then Frankfurt. Cantor excelled in school where he developed lifelong interests in philosophy, theology, literature, music, and mathematics. He attended three years of high school at the Wiesbaden Gymnasium and spent his final year as a boarder at the Grand-Ducal Realschule in Darmstadt, where he graduated in 1860. Although Cantor expressed a strong interest in becoming a mathematician, his father insisted that he pursue a career in engineering. After two years in the engineering program at Höheren Gewerbschule, a technical college in Darmstadt, he persuaded his parents to allow him to study mathematics at Polytechnikum Institute (Polytechnic Institute) in Zurich, Switzerland.

When his father died of tuberculosis in 1863, Cantor transferred to the University of Berlin, where he had the opportunity to study with Karl Weierstrass, Eduard Kummer, and Leopold Kronecker, three of the leading mathematicians in Europe. To broaden his mathematical experience, he spent the summer semester of 1866 at the University of Göttingen. In December 1867 he presented his doctoral dissertation "De aequationibus secundi gradus indeterminatis" (On indeterminate equations of the second degree). In this work Cantor solved an open problem that German mathematician Carl Friedrich Gauss had identified in 1801 regarding the integers x, y, and z that satisfy equations of the form $ax^2 + by^2 + cz^2 = 0$ for arbitrary integer coefficients a, b, and c. The solution of this difficult problem earned him his doctoral degree with the distinction magna cum laude (high honors). In that same year Cantor wrote another thesis titled *In re mathematica ars propendi pluris facienda est quam solvendi* (In mathematics the art of asking questions is more valuable than solving problems) that foreshadowed the significance of his career in which the questions he raised and left unanswered led to greater achievements than the theorems that he succeeded in proving.

While waiting to obtain a position as a university professor, Cantor passed the *Staatsprüfung* (national examination), the German certification test for school teachers, and taught for a year at a girls' school in Berlin. In 1869 he accepted a position at the University of Halle as a *Privatdozent* (assistant professor) meaning that he could lecture at the university but collected his fees directly from his students. He advanced in rank becoming an *Extraordinarius* (associate professor) in 1872 and an *Ordinariat* (full professor) in 1879. Although he continually sought positions at more prestigious institutions where he could teach better students and collaborate with more accomplished research mathematicians, he spent his entire 44-year academic career at the University of Halle. In 1874 Cantor married his sister's friend Vally Guttmann, with whom he had two sons and four daughters.

Research in Analysis and Number Theory

As a protégé of Kummer and Weierstrass, Cantor did his early mathematical research in analysis and number theory, the same areas as his former teachers. Working with Heinrich Heine, the leading mathematician at the University of Halle, he became particularly interested in questions relating to Fourier series, a method for representing functions as infinite sums of sines and cosines. The 10 papers that he wrote between 1867 and 1873 demonstrated his ability to conduct high-quality research and established him as a serious and gifted mathematician.

Cantor presented his most significant work from this period in his 1872 paper titled "Über die Ausdehnung eines Satzes aus der Theorie der trignometrischen Reihen" (On the generalization of a theorem from the theory of trigonometric series), which appeared in the journal *Mathematische Annalen* (Annals of mathematics). In this paper he constructed the real numbers as the limits of fundamental sequences (now called Cauchy sequences) of rational numbers. According to his definition, if two such sequences of rational numbers $a_1, a_2, a_3, \ldots$ and $b_1, b_2, b_3, \ldots$ both had the same limit and the sequence of their differences $a_1 - b_1, a_2 - b_2, a_3 - b_3, \ldots$ converged to zero, then the sequences were equivalent and they represented the same real number. Although mathematicians had been working with real numbers for thousands of years, Cantor's construction provided the first concrete representation of the concept of real number. In the same year another German mathematician, Richard Dedekind, published his concept of Dedekind cuts that defined a real number as the boundary value separating all the rational numbers that were less than it from all the rational numbers that were greater than it. The two equivalent concepts that they developed independently form the Cantor-Dedekind axiom of real numbers, a fundamental concept in analysis.

In his work with real numbers Cantor presented infinite series of the form $c_1 + \dfrac{c_2}{2!} + \dfrac{c_3}{3!} + \dfrac{c_4}{4!} + \ldots$ where the numerators were non-negative integers. He proved that any positive real number could be represented as the limit of the sequence of partial sums of these series that are now known as Cantor series. He also investigated the representation of real numbers as infinite products. The partial products formed by the first n terms provided further sequences for defining real numbers.

Through their research on the topic of real numbers, Dedekind and Cantor established a mutually advantageous working relationship and a deep friendship. While in Switzerland on his honeymoon in 1874, Cantor spent time discussing mathematics with Dedekind, who was also vacationing there. From 1873 to 1879 the two engaged in a voluminous correspondence about their research.

Dedekind's deep, abstract, logical way of thinking influenced the direction of Cantor's research and the development of his ideas.

The Birth of Set Theory

In their exchange of letters Dedekind and Cantor discussed infinite sets of numbers. Cantor shared his proof that the set of natural numbers (the positive integers) and the set of rational numbers (those numbers that can be written as fractions of two integers) were the same size. He developed a one-to-one correspondence between the two infinite sets by pairing up their elements in a creative manner. First he organized the positive, rational numbers into a collection of rows listing the fractions having denominators of 1, followed by the fractions having denominators of 2, the fractions having denominators of 3, and so on. He then linked these numbers into a sequence $\frac{1}{1}, \frac{2}{1}, \frac{1}{2}, \frac{1}{3}, \frac{2}{2}, \frac{3}{1}, \frac{4}{1}, \frac{3}{2}, \frac{2}{3}, \frac{1}{4}, \frac{1}{5}, \frac{2}{4}, \frac{3}{3}, \frac{4}{2}, \frac{5}{1}, \ldots$ by going up the first diagonal, down the second, up the third, down the fourth, and so on. Ignoring duplicate entries such as $\frac{2}{2}, \frac{2}{4}, \frac{3}{3},$ and $\frac{4}{2}$ whose values had occurred earlier in the list as fractions reduced to their lowest terms, he managed to assign a distinct natural number to each positive, rational number. Inserting the negative of each value after the corresponding positive entry and listing zero as the initial value, his innovative diagonal argument proved that the set of rational numbers was a countably infinite set. He became well known for the various types of diagonal arguments that he used to prove several important results throughout his career.

Cantor was not the first mathematician to notice that it was possible to establish a one-to-one correspondence between the members of an infinite set and the elements of one of its subsets. In 1632 Italian scientist Galileo Galilei had observed that the natural numbers 1, 2, 3, 4, 5, . . . could be paired with the seemingly smaller collection of square numbers $1^2 = 1$, $2^2 = 4$, $3^2 = 9$, $4^2 = 16$, $5^2 = 25$, . . . Although only some natural numbers were squares, this pairing suggested that the collection of squares was as numerous as the set of all natural numbers. Puzzled by the apparent contradiction, Galileo did not pursue the subject further. Cantor and Dedekind,

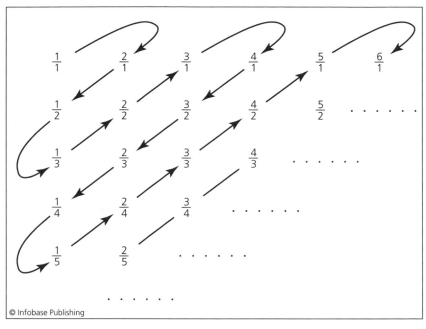

© Infobase Publishing

Using a diagonal argument, Cantor specified a systematic method for listing all positive rational numbers. By ignoring fractions that were not in lowest terms and including zero and negative numbers, he established a one-to-one correspondence between the set of natural numbers and the set of rational numbers.

however, identified this behavior as the defining property of infinite sets. They realized that a set was infinite if its elements could be put into a one-to-one correspondence with the elements of one of its proper subsets—a set that contained some but not all of the elements of the original set.

Cantor formalized and extended his ideas on infinite sets in the paper "Über eine Eigenschaft des Inbegriffes aller reellen algebraischen Zahlen" (On a property of the collection of all real algebraic numbers) that appeared in 1874 in the *Journal für die reine und angewandte Mathematik* (Journal for pure and applied mathematics). In this paper he presented two significant results about infinite sets that radically changed mathematicians' ideas about the concept of infinity. With the publication of this important paper he introduced set theory as a new branch of mathematics.

One of the two major ideas in Cantor's foundational paper dealt with algebraic numbers—those real numbers that were solutions to equations having integer coefficients. Although this set included the <u>natural numbers</u> and the <u>rational numbers</u>, Cantor constructed a one-to-one correspondence between its members and the set of natural numbers. For each polynomial equation $a_0 + a_1x + a_2x^2 + \ldots + a_nx^n = 0$ with integer coefficients he defined its index to be the sum of the absolute values of the coefficients plus the degree of the equation, $|a_0| + |a_1| + \ldots |a_n| + n$. The only equation of index 2 was $x = 0$, so its solution, 0, became the first algebraic number. The four equations of index 3 were $2x = 0$, $x + 1 = 0$, $x - 1 = 0$, and $x^2 = 0$. They had roots 0, –1, 1, so he included the new values –1 and 1 as the second and third entries on his list of algebraic numbers. Cantor observed that for each index there were only finitely many equations and that each equation had only finitely many roots. Listing the new roots by order of index and by increasing magnitude within each index, he established a systematic method for listing all the algebraic numbers. This one-to-one correspondence with the natural numbers proved that the set of algebraic numbers was countably infinite.

The second important result that Cantor proved in this paper was that the set of all real numbers was not countably infinite. He accomplished this by showing that each real number could be identified with a <u>nested sequence of</u> intervals $[a_1, b_1]$, $[a_2, b_2]$, $[a_3, b_3]$, $\ldots$ and that the set of all these sequences could not be put into a one-to-one correspondence with the natural numbers. Several years later, Cantor presented a more elegant diagonal proof that made this result very clear. In his later proof he showed that if the real numbers were countably infinite, then they could be ordered as a sequence of decimal numbers. Given any such sequence, $0.a_1a_2a_3a_4 \ldots$, $0.b_1b_2b_3b_4 \ldots$, $0.c_1c_2c_3c_4 \ldots$, $0.d_1d_2d_3d_4 \ldots$, $\ldots$, he showed that it would always be possible to create a real number that was not in the list by choosing a first digit that was different from a_1, a second digit that was different from b_2, a third digit that was different from c_3, and so on. Since no sequence of numbers could list all real numbers, the set of all real numbers was not countably infinite.

These two results meant that the set of real numbers was somehow significantly larger than the countably infinite sets of natural numbers, rational numbers, and algebraic numbers. Cantor had proved that there were different sizes of infinity—a novel concept

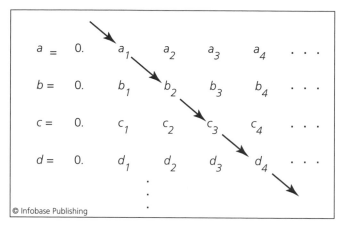

$$a = 0. \quad a_1 \quad a_2 \quad a_3 \quad a_4 \quad \cdots$$

$$b = 0. \quad b_1 \quad b_2 \quad b_3 \quad b_4 \quad \cdots$$

$$c = 0. \quad c_1 \quad c_2 \quad c_3 \quad c_4 \quad \cdots$$

$$d = 0. \quad d_1 \quad d_2 \quad d_3 \quad d_4 \quad \cdots$$

© Infobase Publishing

Cantor proved that no sequence of decimal values could include all real numbers by constructing a number that had a different first digit than the first number in the sequence, a different second digit than the second number in the sequence, and so on. This proof showed that the set of real numbers was not countably infinite and established the existence of different orders of infinity.

that mathematicians had not previously considered. As he became more familiar with these novel ideas, he introduced the terms *power* and *cardinality* to describe the size of a set, called two sets "equipollent" if they had the same cardinality, and created the expression *cardinality of the continuum* to describe the size of the uncountably infinite set of real numbers. In 1844 French mathematician Joseph Liouville had established that there were infinitely many nonalgebraic or transcendental numbers. Cantor's new results meant that the set of transcendental numbers had the cardinality of the continuum. Rather than being rare quantities, they far outnumbered the more familiar algebraic numbers.

Continuum Hypothesis

Cantor continued to investigate the intriguing properties of infinite sets. In his 1878 paper "Ein Beitrag zur Mannigfaltigkeitslehre" (A contribution to manifold theory), which appeared in the *Journal für die reine und angewandte Mathematik*, he proved that a two-dimensional surface and a one-dimensional line had the same number of points. His innovative proof established a one-to-one correspondence between the points in the unit square $S = \{(x,y) \mid 0 \leq x, y \leq 1\}$ and the points in the unit interval $I = \{z \mid 0 \leq z \leq 1\}$. For each point $(x, y) = (0.x_1 x_2 x_3 \ldots, 0.y_1 y_2 y_3 \ldots)$ in the unit square, he merged the digits creating the corresponding point $z = 0.x_1 y_1 x_2 y_2 x_3 y_3 \ldots$ in the unit interval. Conversely, he showed that for any point $z = 0.z_1 z_2 z_3 z_4 z_5 z_6 \ldots$ in the unit interval its digits could be separated, creating two decimal numbers that provided the coordinates of a point $(x, y) = (0.z_1 z_3 z_5 \ldots, 0.z_2 z_4 z_6 \ldots)$ in the unit square. His proof established that, despite their different dimensions, these two sets both had the cardinality of the continuum.

When Cantor completed the proof of this counterintuitive result, he remarked to Dedekind that he saw it but he did not believe it. The implausibility of the result and the fact that his proof technique required an infinite number of steps made his paper highly controversial. Kronecker, who served on the journal's editorial board, tried to prevent its publication and convinced many mathematicians in Germany to reject Cantor's radical ideas. Recognizing the paper's significance, Dedekind successfully argued for it to be published. Cantor was so upset by the reaction to his work that he never submitted any future research results to this journal, even though it was the most prestigious mathematical publication in Europe. Throughout the remainder of his career he had to defend the validity of his innovative ideas and his nonstandard methods.

In the same paper Cantor stated without proof the property that if two infinite sets were not equipollent then one set had to be equipollent to a proper subset of the other. This fundamental principle known as the trichotomy of cardinals seemed obvious to him but, despite repeated attempts, he was unable to prove it. His suggestion of the idea led to productive research by other mathematicians. In 1904 his countryman Ernst Zermello showed that the trichotomy of cardinals could not be proven from the other axioms of set theory because it was independent of them. By introducing an additional principle known as the axiom of choice, Zermello was able to prove the law of trichotomy.

Between 1879 and 1884 Cantor published his most important work on set theory in a six-part treatise titled "Über unendliche, lineare Punktmannichfaltigkeiten" (On infinite, linear manifolds of points) in the journal *Mathematische Annalen*. He stated a principle known as the <u>continuum hypothesis</u>, asserting that every infinite subset of the real numbers was countably infinite or had the cardinality of the continuum. This meant that there were no other types of infinity between these two cardinalities. Using the symbol $\aleph$ (aleph), the first letter of the Hebrew alphabet, he labeled these two orders of infinity as $\aleph_0$ and $\aleph_1$. Cantor attempted to prove and then to disprove the continuum hypothesis but was unable to accomplish either result. In 1900 Russian mathematician David Hilbert identified this conjecture as one of the 23 significant problems that would shape the development of mathematics in the 20th century. His prediction was accurate as attempts by other mathematicians to prove or disprove Cantor's conjecture led to some of the deepest work in set theory. In 1940 Austro-Hungarian mathematician Kurt Gödel confirmed the consistency of the continuum hypothesis by showing that it could not be disproved from the other axioms of set theory. Twenty-three years later, American mathematician Paul Cohen established its independence by showing that the continuum hypothesis could not be proved from the other axioms of set theory. The consistency and independence of Cantor's conjecture meant that it was possible to build valid models of set theory that satisfied the continuum hypothesis and other models that did not. The realization of the existence of this and other unprovable statements changed the nature of mathematics as a rigorous, logical discipline.

In the 1883 installment of this multipart treatise Cantor stated another controversial idea known as the well-ordering principle. He claimed that it was a fundamental property of set theory that every set could be ordered so that each of its subsets had a smallest element. When his critics refused to accept this principle as a basic assumption of set theory, he attempted to prove it but did not succeed. In 1904 Zermello proved that the well-ordering principle was a consequence of his axiom of choice. Eventually mathematicians showed that the axiom of choice, the well-ordering principle, and the trichotomy of cardinals were equivalent, unprovable statements in set theory.

Several of the papers in Cantor's six-part treatise introduced basic ideas such as closed, dense, continuous, and perfect sets that eventually led to the establishment of the branches of mathematics known as point set topology and measure theory. He gave an example of a set now known as the Cantor set that had seemingly inconsistent properties. He constructed this set by starting with the unit interval, removing the middle third (all values between $\frac{1}{3}$ and $\frac{2}{3}$), removing the middle third from the two remaining intervals, and continuing for infinitely many steps, each time removing the middle third from all remaining intervals. He showed that this set consisted of all points in the unit interval that could be written as a sum of the form $\frac{c_1}{3} + \frac{c_2}{3^2} + \frac{c_3}{3^3} + \frac{c_4}{3^4} + \ldots$ where the numerator in each fraction was either 0 or 2. Replacing the denominators in the summations by powers of two and changing any digit of two in the numerators to a one, he showed that the resulting set of points could be put into a one-to-one correspondence with the entire set of points in the unit interval, proving that this nearly empty set had the cardinality of the continuum.

Subset Theorem, Transfinite Arithmetic, and Antinomies

In 1884 Cantor applied for a position on the mathematics faculty at the University of Berlin. Kronecker continued his strong opposi-

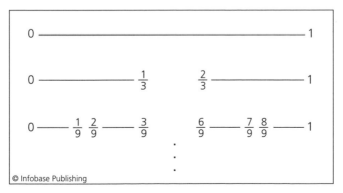

© Infobase Publishing

The Cantor set is the subset of the interval [0, 1] found by removing the middle third of the interval (all values between $\frac{1}{3}$ and $\frac{2}{3}$), removing the middle third from the two remaining intervals, and continuing for infinitely many steps each time removing the middle third from all remaining intervals.

tion to Cantor's ideas and prevented him for obtaining the professorship that he desperately wanted. Cantor responded by writing 52 letters to Gösta Mittag-Leffler, the editor of *Acta Mathematica* (Mathematical activities), attacking Kronecker. In the midst of this controversy Cantor suffered a nervous breakdown and was hospitalized in a mental institution. This was the first of six times that he would be treated at sanatoriums for symptoms of bipolar disorder and manic depression. After being discharged from the hospital, he applied to teach philosophy and literature. He publicly lectured on the theory that Sir Francis Bacon was the real author of Shakespeare's plays.

Despite these challenges, Cantor succeeded in creating national and international networks of mathematicians. He helped to establish the *Deutsche Mathematiker-Vereinigung* (Association of German Mathematicians) in 1890 and served as its first president until 1893. In 1897 he played a prominent role in the organization of the first International Congress of Mathematicians in Zurich. He expended considerable effort promoting the exchange of mathematical ideas among scholars from different institutions and countries.

In the decade of the 1890s Cantor contributed several additional original ideas to the growing field of set theory. In his 1891 paper "Über eine elementare Frage der Mannigfaltigkeitslehre" (On an elementary problem in the study of manifolds) published in the *Jahresbericht der Deutschen Mathematiker-Vereinigung* (Annual Report of the Association of German Mathematicians) he presented his diagonal proof that the real numbers were not a countable set and proved the important subset theorem. For any set S he denoted by $P(S)$ its power set—the collection of all the subsets of S. In the subset theorem Cantor showed that for any infinite set S its power set $P(S)$ had a larger cardinality than S. Generalizing his earlier theorem on the cardinality of the continuum where he proved that there were at least two different sizes of infinity, the subset theorem also known as Cantor's theorem established the fact that there were infinitely many cardinalities, which he called transfinite numbers.

Cantor's final mathematical treatise "Beiträge zur Begründung der transfiniten Mengenlehre" (Contributions to the foundation of the study of transfinite sets) was published in two parts in 1895 and 1897 in the journal *Mathematische Annalen*. Philip Jourdain's

English translation of this pair of papers appeared in book form in 1915. In this treatise he developed rules for arithmetic with transfinite numbers, showing how to add and multiply infinite quantities. He also introduced without proof the principle that for two infinite sets A and B, if A has the same cardinality as a subset of B and B has the same cardinality as a subset of A, then A and B must have the same cardinality. Felix Bernstein in 1896 and Ernst Schröder in 1898 independently developed proofs of this principle, which is now known as the Cantor-Schröder-Bernstein equivalence theorem. In addition to introducing new ideas on transfinite numbers, Cantor's comprehensive treatise presented a polished summary of his 20 years of work on the development of set theory.

While writing this treatise, Cantor discovered several seemingly contradictory results that he called antinomies or paradoxes. In an 1896 letter to Hilbert he posed one of these antinomies about the set of all sets. Cantor suggested that since this was the largest possible set its cardinality would be the largest possible cardinal but, as he had proved earlier, its power set would have an even larger cardinality. Neither Hilbert nor Cantor could settle the apparent inconsistency of this problem. Mathematical logicians later resolved the issue by redefining the rules of set theory to preclude the existence of a set of all sets.

Cantor spent his final 20 years defending his controversial theory of sets and the validity of his methods of proof against criticism from other German mathematicians. Beyond the borders of his own country, his international colleagues admired his work. He became an honorary member of the London Mathematical Society in England and the Mathematical Society of Kharkov in Russia. He received honorary degrees from Christiania University in Norway and St. Andrew's School in Scotland. Cantor's mental and physical health deteriorated, requiring more frequent periods of hospitalization. He died on January 6, 1918, at Halle University's psychiatric clinic.

Conclusion

After his death Cantor's ideas about infinite sets gained strong support throughout the mathematical community. His idea of set became a unifying concept underlying all branches of mathematics and led to the development of the new fields of topology, measure theory, and set theory. At the Second International Congress of Mathematicians in Paris in 1900 Hilbert identified Cantor's continuum hypothesis as the first of 23 problems that would be central to the development of mathematics in the 20th century. The subsequent research on the continuum hypothesis, the well-ordering principle, the trichotomy of cardinalities, and the set of all sets played important roles in the establishment of a rigorous theory of sets. Geometers have constructed fractal images such as the Sierpinski carpet and the Menger sponge that form two- and three-dimensional generalizations of the Cantor set. Mathematical logicians and number theorists continue to model their proofs on Cantor's elegant diagonal method.

FURTHER READING

Ashurst, F. Gareth. "Georg Cantor." In *Founders of Modern Mathematics*, 69–82. London: Muller, 1982. Chapter 6 discusses Cantor's life and his mathematical contributions.

Buskes, Gerard J. "Georg Cantor 1845–1918 Russian-Born German Algebraist and Analyst." In *Notable Mathematicians from Ancient Times to the Present*, edited by Robin V. Young, 91–93. Detroit, Mich.: Gale, 1998. Brief but informative description of his life and work.

Dauben, Joseph Warren. *Georg Cantor: His Mathematics and Philosophy of the Infinite*. Princeton, N.J.: Princeton University Press, 1990. Updated version of the 1979 book-length biography, heavily mathematical.

Dunham, William. "The NonDenumerability of the Continuum." and "Cantor and the Transfinite Realm." In *Journey Through Genius: The Great Theorems of Mathematics*. 245–283. New York: Wiley, 1994. Chapters 11 and 12 discuss Cantor's work with the concept of the infinite in an historical context.

Eves, Howard. "Beyond the Finite." In *Great Moments in Mathematics (after 1650)*, 159–170. Lecture 34 discusses the significance of Cantor's theory of transfinite numbers.

Gray, Robert. "Georg Cantor and Transcendental Numbers." *American Mathematical Monthly* 101 no. 9 (1994): 819–832. Article from mathematical journal detailing Cantor's proof about the cardinality of the set of transcendental real numbers.

Henderson, Harry. "Georg Cantor (1845–1918)." In *Modern Mathematicians*, 26–35. New York: Facts On File, 1996. Brief biographical profile discussing his life and work.

James, Ioan. "Georg Cantor (1845–1918)." In *Remarkable Mathematicians from Euler to von Neumann*, 208–215. Washington, D.C.: Mathematical Association of America, 2003. Brief biography and description of his mathematics.

Meschkowski, H. "Cantor, Georg." In *Dictionary of Scientific Biography*, vol. 3, edited by Charles C. Gillispie, 52–58. New York: Scribner, 1972. Encyclopedic biography including a detailed description of his mathematical writings.

Muir, Jane. "Georg Cantor." In *Of Men and Numbers, the Story of the Great Mathematicians*, 217–240. New York: Dover, 1996. Biographical sketch and assessment of his mathematics.

O'Connor, J. J., and E. F. Robertson. "Georg Ferdinand Ludwig Phillip Cantor." In "MacTutor History of Mathematics Archive." University of Saint Andrews. Available online. URL: http://www-groups.dcs.st-andrews.ac.uk/~history/Mathematicians/Cantor.html. Accessed on March 17, 2003. Online biography, from the University of Saint Andrews, Scotland.

Rowe, David E., and John McCleary, editors. *The History of Mathematics Volume I: Ideas and Their Reception.* Boston: Academic Press, 1989. Includes essays on Cantor's views on the foundations of mathematics and a history of the continuum problem.

9

Sonya Kovalevsky

(1850–1891)

Sonya Kovalevsky, one of the first women to receive a doctoral degree in mathematics, discovered one of the fundamental principles of partial differential equations and won first prize in an international mathematics competition for her analysis of rotating objects.
(*Courtesy of the Library of Congress*)

Pioneering Woman Mathematician

Sonya Kovalevsky (pronounced ko-va-LEV-skee) broke gender barriers in mathematics by becoming one of the first women to receive a doctoral degree in mathematics and to be appointed as a university professor. In her first research paper she discovered one of the fundamental principles of partial differential equations. Her analysis of the rotation of an asymmetric object called the

Kovalevsky top won first prize in an international mathematics competition. She also discovered properties of elliptic integrals, the ring of Saturn, and the bending of light as it passes through crystals.

Kovalevsky's name has been translated in a number of different ways from her native Russian alphabet and has been reported in different forms in various sources. Her first name is sometimes given as Sonya or Sonia and at other times as Sophia, Sofia, or Sofya. Her last name appears as Kovalevsky, Kovalevskaya, or Kovalevskaia.

Early Mathematical Influences

Sonya Vasilevna Krukovsky was born on January 15, 1850, in Moscow, Russia, to parents who were educated members of the upper class of Russian society. Vasily Krukovsky, her father, was an artillery general in the Russian army, whose military rank and substantial income afforded the Krukovsky family a comfortable lifestyle. Velizaveta Schubert, her mother, was an educated woman from a prosperous family. Her grandfather, Fyodor Fyodorovich Schubert, had been a mathematician in charge of the army's mapmaking division and her great-grandfather, Fyodor Ivanovich Schubert, had been a mathematician and a noted astronomer.

Sonya was the middle child in a family of three children. Competing with her older sister, Anuita, and her younger brother, Feyda, for their parents' affection and attention, she became focused on personal achievements. Through the harsh discipline of her governesses and nannies, she became a perfectionist. At the family's rural estate in the town of Palibino, where she had few playmates, Sonya developed a vivid imagination. This aspect of her childhood developed characteristics of her personality that served her well in her mathematical career.

During her childhood and teenage years five major influences stimulated Sonya's interest in mathematics. When her parents redecorated the family's house, the workers did not have enough wallpaper to finish her room, so they papered some of her walls with copies of lecture notes from a calculus book that her father had used as a young student. She spent many hours trying to understand the strange words and symbols on her walls and attempting to determine the proper ordering of the pages. Although she did not understand the meaning of the mathematics, she memorized many of the formulas and symbols.

Sonya's uncle Peter Krukovsky introduced her to interesting mathematical ideas such as the problem of constructing a square and a circle, both having the same area, and the concept of curves that approach a straight line without touching it. His enthusiasm and respect for mathematics stirred Sonya's imagination and sparked her interest in the subject.

The Krukovskys hired tutors to teach their three children a broad range of subjects. Although she enjoyed learning about history, literature, and foreign languages, Sonya devoted most of her time to her math lessons. When her father discovered that she was neglecting her other subjects, he ordered the tutor to stop teaching her mathematics. Defiantly, Sonya secretly borrowed an algebra book and studied at night while her family slept.

When the Krukovskys' neighbor Professor N. N. Tyrtov gave the family a copy of a physics textbook that he had written, Sonya read it with great interest. Although her tutoring sessions had not included any trigonometry, she reconstructed the proper meaning of the sine and cosine functions as ratios of distances between points on a circle. Recognizing Sonya's profound ability and interest, Professor Tyrtov tried to persuade her father to let Sonya pursue further study in mathematics.

When she was 15 years old, her father reluctantly agreed to let her travel to the naval school in St. Petersburg to take a calculus course from Alexander Strannoliubsky, a respected professor of mathematics. Amazed by her rapid mastery of the subject, he asked if she had previously studied calculus. Sonya explained that since she had already memorized the formulas from her wallpaper, she needed only an explanation of their meaning.

Mathematical Studies in Germany

Sonya and her sister, Anuita, wanted to study at universities and travel to Europe. In the 1860s Russian universities did not admit female students, and Russian women were not allowed to travel to foreign countries unless they were accompanied by their husbands or male family members. Determined to study and travel, the two sisters arranged for Sonya to marry Vladimir Kovalevsky, a student at Moscow University and an idealistic revolutionary who sympathized with their plans. To obtain her father's blessing on the marriage, Sonya sent a note to her parents during a dinner party announcing her intention to marry Vladimir. When the party guests learned of Sonya's engagement, her father was forced to agree to the marriage rather than be publicly embarrassed by the rebelliousness of his daughter. In September 1868, 18-year-old Sonya Krukovsky married 26-year-old Vladimir Kovalevsky.

In the spring of 1869 the three traveled to Europe to pursue university educations—Anuita to Paris, France; Vladimir to Vienna, Austria; Sonya to Heidelberg, Germany. At Heidelberg University, Germany's oldest and most respected university, women could not formally enroll in courses, but Kovalevsky obtained permission from several professors who allowed her to attend their lectures. Mathematics professor Leo Königsberger informally directed her studies for a year and a half. Recognizing that she possessed exceptional mathematical talents, he recommended that she attend Berlin University to study with his former professor and research director, Karl Weierstrass.

In August 1870 Kovalevsky arrived in Berlin with letters of recommendation from her professors in Heidelberg to meet Weierstrass. To assess her abilities, he gave her a set of difficult math problems, which she solved in just one week. Her clever and clear solutions so impressed Weierstrass that he insisted she study with him. Berlin University, like Heidelberg, did not allow women to register for classes officially. Although he was known as the father of mathematical analysis and was one of Europe's leading mathematicians, Weierstrass was unable to persuade the university to make an exception for Kovalevsky. He agreed to tutor her privately.

Important Discovery in Differential Equations

For four years Kovalevsky read Weierstrass's lecture notes and met with him to review any details that she did not understand. She read his published and unpublished research papers and discussed the latest theories of geometry and <u>functional analysis</u> with him. Under his direction she worked on several research projects and wrote up her results in three major papers.

Kovalevsky's first research paper was titled "Zur Theorie der partiellen Differentialgleichungen" (Toward a theory of partial differential equations). Differential equations provide mathematical descriptions of the rate at which one quantity changes compared to another quantity such as the rate at which a company's profit will change as it raises the price of its product or the rate at which the population of fish in a lake will increase or decrease as the water temperature changes. Weierstrass had previously published some work about rates of change for situations involving one variable. French mathematician Augustin-Louis Cauchy extended this work to situations involving many variables. Kovalevsky completed the project by identifying the conditions under which a partial differential equation would have a solution and determining when that solution would be the only solution.

This paper on the existence and uniqueness of solutions made a major contribution to the field of differential equations and appeared in 1875 as the lead article in Germany's leading mathematics journal *Journal für die reine und angewandte Mathematik* (Journal for pure and applied mathematics). The work drew immediate praise from other mathematical researchers. Charles Hermite called it the point of departure for all future research on the subject. Henri Poincaré regarded it as a significant improvement over Cauchy's method of proof. This result has come to be known as the <u>Cauchy-Kovalevsky theorem</u> and remains a basic principle in the theory of partial differential equations.

Kovalevsky's second research paper was titled "Über die Reduction einer bestimmten Klasse von Abel'scher Integrale 3-en Ranges auf elliptische Integrale" (On the reduction of a definite class of Abelian integrals of the third range). This paper extended one of Weierstrass's results in an area of advanced calculus and showed how to convert certain types of expressions called Abelian integrals to simpler elliptic integrals, making those difficult problems easier to solve. The paper eventually appeared in 1884 in the journal *Acta Mathematica* (Mathematical activities).

Her third paper was "Zusätse und Bemerkungen zu Laplace's Untersuchung über die Gestalt des Saturnringes" (Supplementary research and observations on Laplace's research on the form of the Saturn ring). The French mathematician Pierre-Simon Laplace had proposed a revolutionary theory about the formation of the Sun and the planets. Kovalevsky gave mathematical explanations for some of the properties of the thick ring of ice and rocks that orbits around the equator of the planet Saturn. She proved that the ring was not a circle or an ellipse but was more egg-shaped and that its shape was continuously changing. In this research Kovalevsky introduced a novel way to use mathematical objects known as power series. Adapting this approach, Poincaré and other mathematicians applied her power series method to additional problems. While her first two papers addressed topics in more abstract areas of mathematics, this research paper demonstrated Kovalevsky's ability to solve problems in applied mathematics and science. It was eventually published in 1885 in the journal *Astronomische Nachrichten* (Astronomical news).

After four years of productive work, Weierstrass felt that Kovalevsky's research was sufficient to earn her a Ph.D. in mathematics. Because she was not enrolled as a student at Berlin

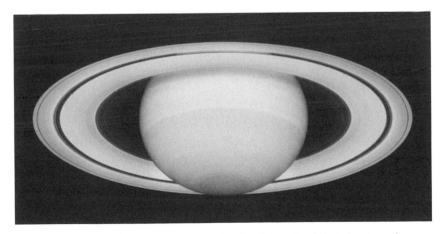

Using the method of power series, Kovalevsky determined that the ring of Saturn was not a circle or an ellipse but was more egg-shaped and that its shape was continuously changing. *(Courtesy of the National Aeronautics and Space Administration)*

University, the university's officials refused to grant her a doctoral degree. Weierstrass contacted his colleagues at the nearby University of Göttingen, who reviewed her work and found it to be of the highest quality. In August 1874, when the University of Göttingen awarded Sonya Kovalevsky a doctorate in mathematics summa cum laude (with highest honors), she became the first woman outside of Renaissance Italy to earn a doctorate in mathematics.

Mathematics Professor

Although Kovalevsky's work in differential equations and her extraordinary accomplishments as a woman in mathematics were well known throughout the mathematical community, no European university would appoint a woman to a faculty position. She encountered the same discriminatory practices as she applied for positions teaching mathematics in Russian gymnasiums, the equivalent of American high schools. Her husband, Vladimir, who had received his doctorate from Austria's Jena University in paleontology, the study of fossils, was also unable to obtain a teaching position. Disappointed and discouraged, the couple moved back to Russia to rejoin her family.

During the next four years Kovalevsky engaged in nonmathematical activities. When her father died in 1875, she and Vladimir moved to St. Petersburg, where they enjoyed an active social life and attempted a variety of business enterprises, including ventures in publishing, real estate, and oil. *Novoe vremia* (New times), a newspaper run by her husband, published four of her articles on popular science themes and many of her reviews of theater productions. She wrote poetry, a novel entitled *The University Lecturer*, and many articles about women's rights. Serving as a member of the fund-raising committee, she helped to establish Higher Women's Courses, a college for women in St. Petersburg, yet was not invited to join the faculty. On October 17, 1878, Kovalevsky gave birth to her only child, a daughter named Sofya Vladimirovna, affectionately called Fufa.

Soon after her daughter's birth, Kovalevsky turned her attention back to mathematics. She translated her paper on Abelian integrals into Russian and in 1879 presented it at a Russian mathematical and scientific conference, the Sixth Congress of Naturalists and Physicians, in St. Petersburg. Even though the research was six years old, mathematicians at the conference praised the paper and encouraged Kovalevsky to pursue her mathematical interests. She attended meetings of the Moscow Mathematical Society and, on March 29, 1881, this group of professional mathematicians elected her as a member. After spending 10 months in Berlin conducting research with Weierstrass on light waves and crystals, Kovalevsky moved to Paris, where she quickly became active within the French community of mathematicians. The Paris Mathematical Society admitted her as an official member in July 1882. Although she was deeply affected by her husband's suicide in April 1883, Kovalevsky continued her mathematical research on the refraction of light waves in a crystalline medium. In August 1883 she presented a paper on this topic at the Seventh Congress of Naturalists and Physicians in Odessa, Russia.

In the fall of 1883 Kovalevsky finally obtained a teaching position at the University of Stockholm, a progressive institution in Sweden that had been established in 1879 to educate both men and women. The university's director, mathematician Gösta Mittag-Leffler, who, like Kovalevsky, had studied with Weierstrass, wanted his institution to be the first in Europe to have a distinguished female mathematician on its faculty. Due to opposition from other faculty members, he was only able to offer Kovalevsky a one-year position at the lowest faculty rank of *Privatdozent* (assistant professor), which meant that she could lecture at the university but would have to collect her fees directly from her students rather than receive a salary from the institution.

Research on Light Waves

During the next seven years Kovalevsky progressed from this marginal appointment to become an active, recognized, and respected member of the European mathematical community. The hundreds of faculty members and students who attended her first classroom lecture on differential equations applauded at its conclusion. Within six months she learned enough Swedish to teach the students in their native language. By the end of her first year, Mittag-Leffler had raised enough money from private donations to offer her a five-year appointment as an "extraordinary" or assistant professor, making her the first female mathematician to hold a regular faculty appointment at a European university in more than 100 years. When *Acta Mathematica* appointed her to their editorial board, she became the first woman to serve as an editor of a major scientific journal. In this new role she read research papers submitted by mathematicians from many countries and helped to organize conferences throughout Europe.

Kovalevsky continued her research on light waves and published her results in three mathematical journals. In 1884 the prominent French scientific journal *Comptes rendus hebdomadaires de l'Academie des Sciences* (Weekly rendering of the accounts of the Academy of Sciences) published a brief summary of her research in the paper "Sur la propagation de la lumière dans un milieu cristallisé" (On the propagation of light in a crystalline medium). A similar summary titled "Om ljusets fortplannting uti ett kristalliniskt medium" (On the refraction of light in a crystalline medium) appeared in 1884 in the Swedish journal *Öfversigt Akademiens Forhandlinger* (Overview of academic achievements). The next year the German journal *Acta Mathematica* published her full 55-page research report entitled "Über die Brechung des Lichtes in cristallinischen Mitteln" (On the refraction of light in a crystal medium).

Prize-Winning Work on Rotation of Kovalevsky Top

In 1888 Kovalevsky entered the competition for the *Prix Bordin* (Bordin Prize) offered by the French Academy of Sciences. The competition required contestants to investigate the rotation of a solid object around a fixed point. Kovalevsky had been interested in this topic since the start of her mathematical career and had been actively researching it since 1884. Some examples of this type of motion are a spinning top, a gyroscope, and the pendulum of a clock. Many famous mathematicians, including Leonhard Euler,

Joseph-Louis Lagrange, Siméon-Denis Poisson, and Carl Jacobi had worked on this problem in the previous 100 years and had described two possible types of rotation. Kovalevsky discovered that an object that is not symmetrical could turn in a third way. The irregular spinning object that she investigated became known as the Kovalevsky top. Her elegant solution to this difficult problem easily won the competition. The judges considered her entry to be such an extraordinary contribution to mathematical physics that they increased the prize money from 3,000 to 5,000 francs. On Christmas Eve, 1888, she was awarded the Bordin Prize before a gathering of the best mathematicians and scientists in France. She was only the second woman to receive a significant prize from the French Academy of Sciences.

Acta Mathematica published Kovalevksy's solution in the paper "Sur le problème de la rotation d'un corps solide autour d'un point fixe" (On the problem of the rotation of a solid body about a fixed point) in 1889. Her continued research on this problem led to two additional research papers. "Sur une propriété du système d'équations différentielles qui définit la rotation d'un corps solide autour d'un point fixe" (On a property of the system of differential equations that define the rotation of a solid body about a fixed point) appeared in *Acta Mathematica* in 1890. "Mémoire sur un cas particulier du problème de la rotation d'un corps pesant autour d'un point fixe, où l'intégration s'effectue à l'aide de fonctions ultraelliptiques du temps" (Report on a particular case of the problem of the rotation of a heavy body about a fixed point, where the integration is accomplished with the use of hyperelliptic functions of time) was printed as the 62-page lead article in the 1894 edition of *Mémoires présentés par divers savants à l'Académie des Sciences de l'institute national de France* (Reports presented by various scholars to the Academy of Sciences of the National Institute of France).

Kovalevsky's work on the rotation problem had a significant influence on research in the area of mathematical physics. Mathematicians from many European countries praised her adept use of complex analysis, Abelian functions, and hyperelliptic integrals as well as her simple, direct, and complete analysis of the general problem. Russian mathematician N. E. Zhukovski recommended that her excellent analysis be included as a standard component of all university level analytical mechanics courses. More than 100 years later, mathematical physicists continue to use the asymptotic method that she employed. Her analysis of the problem was so complete that, even though the rotation problem continues to be studied today, no new cases have been discovered.

The Bordin Prize was the first of many ways that the European mathematical community honored Kovalevsky for her work on the rotation problem. In 1889 the Stockholm Academy of Sciences awarded her a prize of 1,500 kroner. That same year the French Ministry of Education named her an "officer of public instruction," an honorary title indicating the respect she had earned within that country's mathematical community. In June 1889 the University of Stockholm made her a permanent member of their faculty by appointing her to the position of professor of mathematics with tenure. No other woman had held a tenured appointment at a European university since the Italian Renaissance. On December 2, 1889, she became the first woman to be elected as a corresponding member of Russia's Imperial Academy of Sciences. Although she hoped that this recognition signaled a shift in Russian society, this honorary title did not permit her to attend meetings of the academy and did not lead to the offer of a teaching position at a Russian university.

Novelist and Playwright

In addition to her mathematical research, Kovalevsky maintained a lifelong interest in literature and the performing arts. Since her childhood when she and her sister, Anuita, became friends with Russian novelist Fyodor Dostoyevsky, she had developed friendships with many European writers and had written novels and plays dealing with social rebellion. Her short novel *Vera Vorontsova* (A nihilist girl) depicted Russian life during the social revolution of the 1870s. Her autobiography *Recollections of Childhood*, describing her life as a young girl growing up in Russia, was published in Russian, Swedish, and Danish. A fictionalized account of this book titled *From Russian Life: The Sisters Rayevsky* appeared in 1890 in two issues of the Russian magazine *Vestnik Evropy* (European messenger). Both versions received enthusiastic reviews from literary critics who compared them to the best Russian literature of the time. During her years in Sweden Kovalevsky and Mittag-Leffler's sister Anna Carlotta Leffler cowrote a pair of plays titled *A Struggle for Happiness: How It Was and How It Might Have Been*, which were performed in Sweden and Russia in 1890.

Kovalevsky made her final contribution to mathematics in 1890, when she discovered a simplified proof of a theorem from potential theory that physicist Heinrich Bruns had proven earlier. Her short paper on this subject, "Sur un théorème de M. Bruns" (On a theorem by Mr. Bruns), appeared in 1891 in *Acta Mathematica*.

While returning to Sweden from a vacation on the French Riviera, Kovalevsky was caught in a winter storm and became seriously ill with pneumonia and the flu. Six days later, on February 10, 1891, she died at the age of 41. She was buried in Sweden, her adopted country.

Conclusion

During her career Sonya Kovalevsky made two significant contributions to mathematical research. The Cauchy-Kovalevsky Theorem is a fundamental result in the area of partial differential equations. Her research on the rotation problem and the Kovalevsky top remains the most advanced work on this subject. Through her many achievements as a student, professor, editor, and researcher, she demonstrated to a male-dominated mathematical community that women were capable of understanding and contributing to the field of mathematics.

Shortly after her death, the Higher Women's Courses, the college for women in St. Petersburg that Kovalevsky helped to establish, raised money for a scholarship to be given in her name. To honor her memory, the Russian post office issued a stamp displaying her picture. As a living tribute, every year since 1985 the Association for Women in Mathematics has sponsored Sonya Kovalevsky Mathematics Days, during which high school girls participate in workshops, presentations, and problem-solving competitions.

FURTHER READING

Beal, Susan. "Sofya Korvin-Krukovskaya Kovalevskaya." In *Notable Women in Mathematics: A Biographical Dictionary*, edited by Charlene Morrow and Teri Perl, 102–107. Westport, Conn.: Greenwood, 1998. Short biographical sketch.

Henderson, Harry. "Sofia Kovalevskaia (1850–1891)." In *Modern Mathematicians*, 36–45. New York: Facts On File, 1996. Biographical profile.

James, Ioan. "Sonya Kovalevskaya (1850–1891)." In *Remarkable Mathematicians from Euler to von Neumann*, 230–237. Washington, D.C.: Mathematical Association of America, 2003. Brief biography and description of her mathematics.

Koblitz, Ann Hibner. *A Convergence of Lives Sofia Kovalevskaia: Scientist, Writer, Revolutionary*. New Brunswick, N.J.: Rutgers University Press, 1993. Book-length biography.

———. "Sofia Vasilevna Kovalevskaia (1850–1891)." In *Women of Mathematics: A Biobibliographic Sourcebook*, edited by Louise S. Grinstein and Paul J. Campbell, 103–113. New York: Greenwood, 1987. Biographical profile with an evaluation of her mathematics and an extensive list of references.

Kramer, Edna E. "Kovalevsky, Sonya." In *Dictionary of Scientific Biography*, vol. 7, edited by Charles C. Gillispie, 477–480. New York: Scribner, 1972. Encyclopedic biography and description of her mathematical writings.

O'Connor, J. J., and E. F. Robertson. "Sofia Vasilyevna Kovalevskaya." In "MacTutor History of Mathematics Archive." University of Saint Andrews. Available online. URL: http://www-groups.dcs.st-andrews.ac.uk/~history/Mathematicians/Kovalevskaya.html. Accessed on July 5, 2005. Online biography, from the University of Saint Andrews, Scotland.

Osen, Lynn M. "Sonya Corvin-Krukovsky Kovalevsky." In *Women in Mathematics*, 117–140. Cambridge, Mass.: MIT Press, 1974. Biographical sketch of her life and work.

Perl, Teri. "Sonya Kovalevskaya (1850–1891)." *Math Equals: Biographies of Women Mathematicians + Related Activities*, 126–147. Menlo Park, Calif.: Addison-Wesley, 1978. Biography accompanied by exercises related to her mathematical work.

Reimer, Luetta, and Wilbert Reimer. "The Lessons on the Wall: Sonya Kovalevsky." In *Mathematicians Are People, Too, Stories from the Lives of Great Mathematicians, Volume Two*, 108–117. Parsippany, N.J.: Seymour, 1995. Life story with historical facts and fictionalized dialogue, intended for elementary school students.

Reynolds-Jacquez, Kelley. "Sonya Vasilievna Kovalevskaya (also Transliterated as Sofia Vasilevna Kovalevskaia) 1850–1891 Russian Mathematician and Educator." In *Notable Mathematicians from Ancient Times to the Present*, edited by Robin V. Young, 286–288. Detroit, Mich.: Gale, 1998. Brief but informative description of her life and work.

10

Henri Poincaré

(1854–1912)

In his 500 books and papers Henri
Poincaré introduced algebraic topology, chaos theory, and the theory
of several complex variables as new
branches of mathematics.
(Courtesy of the Library of Congress)

Universal Mathematician

In an era of specialization, Henri Poincaré (pronounced ahn-REE
PWON-kar-ray) was a universalist contributing influential ideas
to many branches of mathematics and physics, including analysis, topology, algebraic geometry, and number theory, as well as
celestial mechanics, fluid mechanics, and the theory of relativity.
In complex analysis he developed the concept of automorphic
functions and introduced the theory of analytic functions of several complex variables. His idea of the fundamental group of a

surface led to the establishment of algebraic topology. Attempts to prove the Poincaré conjecture about the topological properties of a sphere resulted in a century of productive research. In mathematical physics his work on the three-body problem won first prize in an international mathematics competition and established chaos theory. He wrote widely circulated books on celestial mechanics and established two of the basic propositions of the special theory of relativity. The breadth and depth of his accomplishments earned him membership in all five sections of France's Académie des Sciences (Academy of Sciences).

Early Life and Education

Jules-Henri Poincaré was born on April 29, 1854, in the city of Nancy in the Lorraine region of eastern France. Léon Poincaré, his father, was a physician and professor of medicine at the University of Nancy. Eugenie Launois, his mother, was a learned woman who taught him and his younger sister, Aline, to read and write before they attended school. His distinguished relatives included Raymond Poincaré, his cousin, who served as prime minister of France and president of the French Republic during World War I.

Poincaré was a shy, frail child who had poor eyesight and lacked coordination. A bout with diphtheria at the age of five paralyzed his larynx, leaving him unable to speak for nine months. From 1862 to 1873 he attended elementary and high school at the Nancy Lycée, now renamed Lycée Henri Poincaré in his memory. He earned good grades in most of his courses and demonstrated a gift for written composition. During his final year of high school he won first prize in mathematics in the *concours general* (general competition), the national scholastic competition for high school students.

In 1873 Poincaré took the entrance examination for École Polytechnique (Polytechnic University), a university in Paris that provided training in mathematics, science, and engineering, leading to careers in service to the state of France. Although he scored a grade of zero on the drawing portion of the exam, his scores on the other sections of the test were so superior that the examiners made an exception to their rules and admitted him as a student. Consistent with his prior experiences, he struggled with physical exercise, art, and piano playing but excelled in mathematics, writing, and the sciences. Finding it difficult to read the blackboard, he took no notes in lectures, preferring instead to listen, absorb the information, and visualize the concepts. He also developed the abilities to remember material accurately after a single reading and to create well-written compositions without the need for revisions. Under the direction of mathematician Charles Hermite he wrote his first research paper, *Démonstration nouvelle des propriétés de l'indicatrice d'une surface* (New demonstration of the properties of the indicator of a surface), which was published in 1874 in the journal *Nouvelles annales de mathématiques* (New annals of mathematics).

After graduating from École Polytechnique in 1875, Poincaré continued his studies at École des Mines (School of Mines), where he investigated the scientific and commercial methods of the mining industry and continued his study of advanced mathematics. In 1879 he received the degree of ordinary engineer and worked for the Corps des Mines (Forces of the Mines) as an inspector for the Vesoul region of northeastern France. One of his responsibilities during his first year was to investigate the cause of a mine disaster that killed 18 miners in Magny, France. From 1881 to 1885 he worked at the Ministry of Public Services as an engineer in charge of northern railway development. Maintaining a lifelong interest in mining, he rose to the position of chief engineer of the Corps des Mines in 1893 and became inspector general in 1910.

While studying for his degree as a mining engineer, Poincaré also pursued an advanced degree in mathematics. Supervised by Hermite, he wrote a doctoral dissertation titled "Sur les propriétés des functions définies par les équations aux différences partielles" (On properties of functions defined by partial difference equations) in which he studied the geometric properties of functions whose derivatives satisfied specified conditions. The mathematicians who reviewed his thesis remarked favorably on the depth of his analysis. This work earned him a doctorate in mathematics from the University of Pairs in 1879.

After a two-year appointment as a junior lecturer of mathematics at the University of Caen in France, Poincaré joined the faculty at the University of Paris as a professor of mathematical analysis. At various times during his 31-year career at this institution he held the chairs of physical and experimental mechanics, mathematical physics and probability, and celestial mechanics and astronomy. In 1881, the same year that he accepted the appointment in Paris, he married Jeanne-Louise-Marie Poulain d'Andecy. In the next 12 years they had three daughters named Jeanne, Yvonne, and Henriette, and a son, Léon.

Poincaré was a prolific writer, publishing nearly 500 research papers and 30 books during his career. Within the field of mathematics his work contributed to differential equations, algebraic geometry, complex function theory, algebraic topology, number theory, algebra, and probability. His applied research in physics developed ideas in celestial mechanics, mathematical physics, relativity, electromagnetic theory, fluid mechanics, and the theory of light. In several branches of mathematics and physics his research extended for more than a dozen years, overlapping with his work in other areas. At many points in his career he simultaneously worked on five different projects.

Automorphic Functions

One of the most productive areas of Poincaré's early mathematical research was the topic of complex function theory. Between 1881 and 1883 he published 14 papers titled "Sur les fonctions fuchsiennes" (On Fuchsian functions) in *Comptes rendus de l'Académie des Sciences* (Rendering of the accounts of the Academy of Sciences). These papers introduced the class of functions now known as automorphic functions, which could be written as $f(z) = \dfrac{az+b}{cz+d}$. Poincaré called them fuchsian functions after German mathematician Lazarus Fuchs, whose work had led him to their discovery. These functions were the first example of a class of infinitely periodic functions meaning that each such function $f(z)$ had infinitely many constants k for which $f(z) = f(z + k)$. They provided a full generalization of the simply periodic trigonometric functions and the doubly periodic elliptic functions. He established relationships between the algebraic properties of groups of automorphic functions and the geometrical properties of their corresponding fundamental domains.

Poincaré's related paper "Mémoire sur les fonctions fuchsiennes" (Memoir on fuchsian functions) that appeared in 1882 in *Acta Mathematica* (Mathematical activities) introduced a type of infinite summation known as a theta-series that summed all the periods of an automorphic function. His paper analyzed the convergence of such series, the relationships between their derivatives, and the geometric properties of their corresponding domains. In later papers he extended the concepts to thetafuchsian and zetafuchsian functions produced by combinations of automorphic functions and their derivatives. As a result of his extensive research on automorphic functions, Poincaré was elected to the Académie des Sciences (Academy of Sciences) in 1887 at the age of 32.

In his 1883 paper "Sur les functions entières" (On entire functions), which appeared in the *Bulletin de la Société Mathématique de France* (Bulletin of the Mathematical Society of France), Poincaré established several properties of entire functions—functions that have derivatives at all points in the complex plane. He explained how the genus of an entire function, one of its geometrical features, was related to the coefficients of the infinite series that represented the function. He established the general uniformization theorem that specified conditions under which the surface corresponding to an entire function was related to a simpler geometrical surface.

Poincaré extended his research on complex functions to functions involving more than one variable, establishing the basic methods of the theory of functions of several complex variables. With countryman Emile Picard he published the 1883 paper "Sur un théorème de Riemann relatif aux fonctions de n variables indépendantes admettant $2n$ systèmes de périodes" (On a theorem by Riemann relative to functions of n independent variables admitting $2n$ systems of periods) in *Comptes rendus*. In this paper they proved that certain types of functions of two variables known as meromorphic functions could occur only when an entire function is divided by another entire function. In later papers about functions of several complex variables Poincaré studied such concepts as pluriharmonic functions, conformal mappings, and residues of integrals of complex functions. Unlike his work on automorphic functions, Poincaré's contributions to the study of entire functions and functions of several complex variables opened areas of productive research that continues to the present day.

Algebraic Topology

In a series of six papers written between 1895 and 1904 Poincaré created the branch of mathematics known as algebraic topology, in which groups of functions are used to study the properties of geometrical surfaces. His 1895 paper "Analysis Situs" (Positional analysis) appearing in *Journal de l'École Polytechnique* (Journal of the Polytechnic University) gave the original name to the subject that is now known by its more descriptive title, algebraic topology. This paper introduced the concept of a fundamental group of a surface and generalized it to an infinite sequence of related groups known as homotopy groups. In the other five papers bearing similar titles he introduced additional sequences of groups, known as homology and cohomology groups, whose structures corresponded to other features of the surface. He connected these ideas in the Poincaré duality theorem, which established one-to-one correspondences between the kth homology group and the n-kth cohomology group of an n-dimensional surface.

In this series of six publications Poincaré also introduced new methods for analyzing the properties of surfaces that were constructed from simpler geometrical shapes. Using techniques known as triangulation and barycentric subdivision, he proved that every surface had an Euler-Poincaré characteristic—a constant formed by adding and subtracting the number of geometrical shapes of each dimension that comprised the surface. This concept generalized the "edges plus two" formula for polyhedra that Swiss mathematician Leonhard Euler had discovered in the 18th century.

One significant idea Poincaré raised in his set of papers on algebraic topology has come to be known as the Poincaré conjecture. He proved that any two-dimensional surface having the same homotopy, homology, and cohomology groups as the sphere was topologically equivalent to the sphere. In 1900 he conjectured that the same property would hold in all dimensions, but discovered a counterexample for the three-dimensional case. Since that time topologists have proven that the proposed theorem is valid for all dimensions higher than three. Their work on the solution of this difficult problem has led to many new techniques and discoveries in

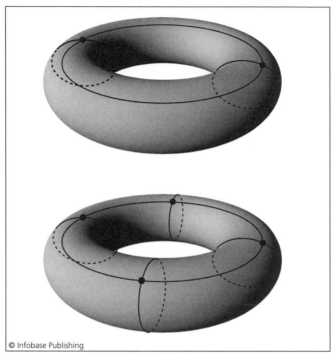

© Infobase Publishing

The Euler-Poincaré characteristic is a topological invariant of a surface. For any triangulation of a particular surface, the alternating sum of the number of components of each dimension produces the same numerical value for the characteristic. These triangulations of a torus into a collection of 2 points, 4 curved line segments, and 2 planar regions and a different collection of 4 points, 8 segments, and 4 regions both give zero as its Euler-Poincaré characteristic since 2 − 4 + 2 = 0 and 4 − 8 + 4 = 0.

the field. In 2000 the Clay Mathematics Institute offered a million-dollar prize for a valid proof of the conjecture. Russian mathematician Grigori Perelman published a paper in 2003 that might have solved the three-dimensional case of the problem; mathematicians are still scrutinizing his methods to determine if his proof is valid.

Contributions to Other Areas of Mathematics

In addition to his research on complex functions and algebraic topology, Poincaré contributed new ideas and techniques to five other areas of mathematics. In almost every year from 1878 to 1912 he wrote at least one paper on differential equations—equations that specify relationships between the derivatives of an unknown function and the function itself. The set of four papers titled "Mémoire sur les courbes définies par une équation différentielle" (Memoir on the curves defined by a differential equation) that appeared between 1880 and 1886 in the *Journal de mathématiques pures et appliquées* (Journal of pure and applied mathematics) advanced the theory of differential equations beyond the limited techniques of integration. The first two papers of the set introduced a qualitative approach to describing the complete set of solutions of a given differential equation. By projecting the x-y plane onto the surface of a sphere, Poincaré was able to analyze the solutions in terms of the number of nodes, saddles, spiral points, and centers—four types of special points where the projected image had particular geometrical features. In the third paper he projected the plane onto more general surfaces and identified an invariant numerical quantity called the genus of the curve whose value was related to the number of nodes, saddles, and spiral points. The fourth paper extended the theory to equations involving higher order derivatives. Poincaré's research on the qualitative approach was so thorough that he developed the complete theory, leaving little for other researchers to contribute. His later papers on differential equations dealt with applications from celestial mechanics.

Between 1881 and 1911 Poincaré published as many pages of research on algebraic geometry as he did on automorphic functions. One focus of this work involved identifying conditions under which groups of Abelian functions could be reduced to a sum of simpler functions. He proved the complete reducibility theorem that showed that Abelian varieties could be decomposed into the sum of simple varieties having finitely many elements in common. His most important contribution to this branch of mathematics was his 1910 paper "Sur les courbes tracées sur les surfaces algébriques" (On curves traced on algebraic surfaces), which appeared in the *Annals de l'École Normale Supérieur* (Annals of the Normal Superior University). In this paper he introduced a technique for representing algebraic curves on a surface as sums of Abelian integrals that were easier to analyze. This technique enabled him to create simpler proofs of some known results and to resolve several open problems in algebraic geometry.

Poincaré published research papers on number theory from 1878 to 1901. Influenced by his thesis adviser, Hermite, his early work presented results on quadratic and cubic forms, including the first general definition of the genus of a form with integer coefficients. His most important work in this area was his 1901 paper "Sur les propriétés arithmétiques des courbes algébriques" (On the arithmetic properties of algebraic curves), which appeared in the *Journal de mathématiques pures et appliqués*. In this paper he solved the Diophantine problem of finding the points (x, y) with rational coordinates that satisfied a polynomial equation having rational coefficients. As the first paper involving algebraic geometry over the field of rational numbers, this work introduced new research techniques for investigating classical problems in number theory.

In the area of algebra two of the many new ideas Poincaré developed were of particular significance. His 1899 paper "Sur les groupes continues" (On continuous groups) published in *Comptes rendus* introduced a concept known as an enveloping algebra and provided a method for constructing its basis. This theorem, now known as the Poincaré-Birkhoff-Witt theorem, has become a fundamental result in the modern theory of Lie algebras. In his 1903 paper "Sur l'intégration algébrique des équations linéaires et les périodes des intégrales abéliennes" (On the algebraic integration of linear equations and the periods of Abelian integrals), which appeared in the *Journal de mathématiques pures et appliqués*, he introduced the important concept of left and right ideals that led to many future developments in ring theory.

As chair of mathematical physics and probability at the University of Paris, Poincaré wrote a number of papers for nonspecialists on the subject of probability theory. His 1907 article "Le hazard" (Chance), which appeared in *Revue du mois* (Review of the month), explained how events that were not predictable as individual occurrences collectively followed patterns that could be described by the laws of probability. For his students at the university he wrote a more formal textbook, *Calcul des probabilités* (Theory of probabilities), in 1896 and published a revised second edition in 1912.

Contributions to Physics

Throughout his career Poincaré applied mathematical techniques to the investigation of many physical phenomena. One of the first questions in applied science that he attempted to resolve was the "three-body problem." This classical situation in celestial mechanics dealt with the positions and motions of three heavenly bodies, such as the Sun, Earth, and the Moon, resulting from their mutual gravitational attraction. In his 1883 paper "Sur certaines solutions particulières du problème des trois corps" (On certain particular solutions of the three-body problem), which was published in the *Bulletin astronomique* (Astronomical bulletin), Poincaré showed that the problem had infinitely many solutions if the mass of the largest body was much greater than the masses of the two smaller ones. In 1887 King Oscar II of Sweden sponsored a competition for the best paper addressing the general *n*-body problem. Two years later, the panel of judges awarded the grand prize to Poincaré for his submission that thoroughly addressed the restricted case of the three-body problem. While reviewing the paper for publication, Gösta Mittag-Leffler, the editor of the journal *Acta Mathematica*, discovered a significant error that led to an incorrect conclusion. In a collection of 50 letters that Poincaré wrote to Mittag-Leffler during the next year he developed a new theory that showed how a slight change in one body's initial position could cause radically different long-term results. The 1890 paper incorporating these ideas titled "Sur le problème des trois corps et les equations de la dynamique" (On the three-body problem and the equations of dynamics) introduced chaos theory, the branch of mathematics that studies the orderly patterns that occur in seemingly random situations. In such mathematical systems, small changes in initial conditions can produce significant variations in outputs.

During his career Poincaré wrote approximately 100 books and papers on celestial mechanics—the branch of physics dealing with the motion of heavenly bodies. His three-volume book *Les méthodes nouvelles de la mécanique céleste* (New methods of celestial mechanics) published between 1892 and 1899 and his three volumes of lecture notes, *Leçons de mécanique céleste* (Lessons on celestial mechanics), published between 1905 and 1911, placed celestial mechanics on a

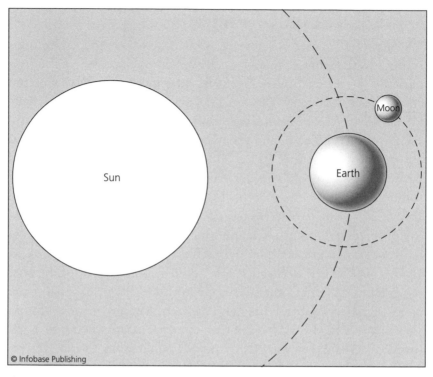

The motions of the Sun, Earth, and Moon determined by their mutual gravitational attraction constitute an example of the three-body problem. Poincaré's research on this topic won first prize in an international mathematics competition and led to the development of chaos theory.

rigorous mathematical basis. In a 130-page paper "Sur l'équilibre d'une masse fluide animée d'un mouvement de rotation" (On the equilibrium of a fluid mass animated by a rotational movement) that was published in *Acta Mathematica* he proved that a rotating fluid such as a star changes its shape from a sphere to an ellipsoid to a pear-shape before breaking into two unequal portions.

Poincaré's research in mathematical physics led him to discover two of the fundamental propositions of the theory of special relativity. In his 1898 paper "La mesure du temps" (The measure of time), which appeared in *Revue de métaphysique et de morale* (Review of metaphysics and ethics), Poincaré formulated the principle that absolute motion did not exist because no mechanical or electromechanical experiment could distinguish between a state of uniform motion and a state of rest. In his 1905 paper "Sur la dynamique de l'électron" (On the dynamics of the electron) he asserted that no object could travel faster than the speed of light. This paper, which appeared in *Comptes rendus* a month before the publication of the first of Albert Einstein's five articles on special relativity, is recognized by physicists as the first paper on the revolutionary theory.

The list of scientific topics that Poincaré researched included almost every aspect of physics. His 70 publications in physics addressed electromagnetic waves, electricity, thermodynamics, optics, potential theory, elasticity, and wireless telegraphs. One of the most influential of these diverse books and articles was his 1896 paper "Les rayons cathodiques et la théorie de Jaumann" (Cathode rays and Jaumann's theory), which appeared in the journal *Eclairage électrique* (Electric lighting). The ideas on the connection between X-rays and phosphorescence that he presented in this paper led French physicist Henri Becquerel to the discovery of radioactivity.

Methods of Research and Popular Science

In 1908 Poincaré gave a lecture titled "L'invention mathématique" (Mathematical invention) at a meeting of Paris's Institut général de psychologie (Institute of General Psychology) in which he shared the thought processes and work habits that led to his major mathematical discoveries. He elaborated on this topic in his widely distributed book *Science and méthode* (*Science and Method*) that appeared later that year. In his presentation and his book he explained that he actively worked on his own research for four hours a day—two hours each morning and two hours each afternoon—and spent his evenings reading mathematical journals. He believed that during the remainder of the day when he appeared to be idle his subconscious mind was working through the information he had absorbed seeking connections and weighing the potential successes of alternative directions of inquiry. According to his theory, discovery resulted from a combination of the conscious application of effort and logical analysis and the equally important subconscious spark of intuition.

Believing that the acquisition of new knowledge depended only partially on logical analysis, Poincaré criticized Welsh mathematician Bertrand Russell and others who were working to reformulate all of mathematics as logical consequences of the basic axioms of set theory. Firmly believing that mathematics had fundamental substance beyond simple logic, he predicted that when future mathematicians looked back upon this era they would be relieved that mathematics had recovered from the disease of set theory.

Despite these harsh words of criticism, Poincaré was an optimistic individual whose works on popular science engaged the literate public and generated interest in current scientific discoveries. His 1902 book *La science et l'hypothèse* (*Science and Hypothesis*) sold 16,000 copies in France during its first 10 years of publication and was translated into 23 other languages. His 1905 book *La valeur de la science* (*The Value of Science*) and the posthumously published *Dernières pensées* (*Last Thoughts*) assembled in 1913 by his family members also conveyed his thoughts on science to wide audiences in many countries.

During his lifetime Poincaré's contemporaries recognized his achievements with a range of honors. In 1889 the French government named him a chevalier de la Légion d'Honneur (knight of the Legion of Honor) in recognition of his work on the three-body problem. France's Académie des Sciences elected him to membership in all five sections of the academy—geometry, mechanics, physics, geography, and navigation—and in 1906 his colleagues elected him as president of the Académie. The literary community of France honored him for the quality of his writings on popular science by electing him to membership in the Académie Française (French Academy), the literary branch of the Institut de France (Institute of France). Dozens of learned societies throughout Europe and America elected him to honorary memberships and many universities awarded him honorary degrees.

Poincaré died at the age of 58 on July 17, 1912, while recovering from surgery for prostate cancer. Royal delegations from many foreign countries and representatives from numerous scholarly societies attended his funeral services. Many people outside the mathematical and scientific community noted his passing.

Conclusion

An ambitious researcher and a prolific writer, Henri Poincaré contributed new ideas and methods to almost every branch of mathematics and physics during his productive 34-year career. He introduced algebraic topology, chaos theory, and the theory of several complex variables as new branches of mathematics. His work with automorphic, entire, and meromorphic functions advanced the study of complex function theory. He developed qualitative techniques in differential equations and introduced left and right ideals in algebra. His thorough analysis of the three-body problem and his pioneering work on fundamental concepts of the special theory of relativity were only two of his many contributions to diverse branches of physics. In the literary field his books on popular science gave the general public a glimpse into the methods of scientific discovery. With his ability to communicate as an equal with specialists from all branches of mathematics and physics, Poincaré was a central figure in the scientific community of his era.

FURTHER READING

Bell, Eric T. "The Last Universalist." In *Men of Mathematics*, 526–554. New York: Simon & Schuster, 1965. Chapter 28 presents an extensive biography and evaluation of his mathematical work.

Dieudonné, Jean. "Poincaré, Jules Henri." In *Dictionary of Scientific Biography*, vol. 11, edited by Charles C. Gillispie, 51–61. New York: Scribner, 1972. Encyclopedic biography including a detailed description of his mathematical writings.

James, Ioan. "Henri Poincaré (1854–1912)." In *Remarkable Mathematicians from Euler to von Neumann*, 237–245. Washington, D.C.: Mathematical Association of America, 2003. Brief biography and description of his mathematics.

Newton, David E. "Jules Henri Poincaré 1854–1912 French Number Theorist, Topologist, and Mathematical Physicist." In *Notable Mathematicians from Ancient Times to the Present*, edited by Robin V. Young, 399–401. Detroit, Mich.: Gale, 1998. Brief but informative description of his life and work.

O'Connor, J. J., and E. F. Robertson. "Jules Henri Poincaré." In "MacTutor History of Mathematics Archive." University of Saint Andrews. Available online. URL: http://www-groups. dcs.st-andrews.ac.uk/~history/Mathematicians/Poincare.html. Accessed on July 6, 2005. Online biography, from the University of Saint Andrews, Scotland.

GLOSSARY

acoustics The study of sound.

aleph The first letter of the Hebrew alphabet, used in set theory to denote different orders of infinity such as $\aleph_0$ (aleph-zero), the cardinality of the NATURAL NUMBERS, and $\aleph_1$ (aleph-one), the cardinality of the REAL NUMBERS.

algebra The branch of mathematics dealing with the manipulation of variables and equations.

algebraic equation A mathematical statement equating two algebraic expressions.

algebraic expression An expression built up out of numbers and variables using the operations of addition, subtraction, multiplication, division, raising to a power, and taking a root.

algebraic number A real number that is the root of a polynomial equation with integer coefficients.

algebraic topology The branch of mathematics in which groups of functions are used to study the properties of geometrical surfaces. Also known as analysis situs.

analysis situs See ALGEBRAIC TOPOLOGY.

Analytical Engine A steam-powered, programmable computing machine that Charles Babbage designed between 1830 and 1870 but never completely built. The machine would have possessed many features of 20th-century electronic computers, including instructions fed in on punched cards, the ability to implement logical branching and condition-controlled looping, and reusable memory locations for variable data.

analytic geometry The algebraic study of geometric curves as a collection of points whose coordinates satisfy an associated equation.

antinomy A situation leading to an apparent logical contradiction; a paradox.

arc The portion of a curve between two specified points.

area diagram A graphical presentation of statistical information in which the area of each region of the diagram is proportional to the value of the corresponding datum.

arithmetic The study of computation.

arithmetic series An infinite sum of the form

$a + (a + r) + (a + 2r) + (a + 3r)+ \ldots$

astronomy The scientific study of stars, planets, and other heavenly bodies.

automorphic function A doubly-periodic, complex function that can be written as $f(z) = \dfrac{az + b}{cz + d}$. Also known as a fuchsian function after German mathematician Lazarus Fuchs.

axiom A statement giving a property of an undefined term or a relationship between undefined terms. The axioms of a specific mathematical theory govern the behavior of the undefined terms in that theory; they are assumed to be true and cannot be proved. Also known as a postulate.

axis A line used to measure coordinates in analytic geometry.

binomial coefficient A positive INTEGER given by the computation $\dbinom{n}{k} = \dfrac{n!}{k! \cdot (n - k)!}$ where n and k are integers satisfying $0 \leq k \leq n$.

binomial theorem The general statement that the sum of two quantities raised to any integer or fractional power can be written as a finite or infinite sum of terms using the generalized binomial coefficients according to the formula

$$(a + b)^n = a^n + \binom{n}{1}a^{n-1}b + \binom{n}{2}a^{n-2}b^2 + \binom{n}{3}a^{n-3}b^3 + \ldots \quad .$$

calculus The branch of mathematics dealing with DERIVATIVES and INTEGRALS.

Cantor set An infinite subset of points formed by removing the middle third of the unit interval, the middle third of each remaining subinterval, and continuing for infinitely many steps.

cardinality A numerical value giving the size of A SET.

cardinality of the continuum A numerical value giving the size of the SET of REAL NUMBERS in the unit interval [0, 1].

celestial mechanics The branch of physics dealing with the motion of heavenly bodies.

central angle An angle formed by two radii of the same circle.

chaos theory The branch of mathematics that studies the orderly patterns that occur in seemingly random situations and mathematical systems in which small changes in initial conditions result in significant variations in outputs.

circle The SET of all points in a plane at a given distance (the radius) from a fixed point (the center).

circumference (1) The points on a circle. (2) The measure of the total arc length of a circle; it is 2π times the radius of the circle.

coefficient A number or known quantity that multiplies a variable in an algebraic expression.

complex number A number that can be written as the sum of a REAL NUMBER and the square root of a negative real number.

composite number A positive INTEGER that can be factored as the product of two or more primes.

computer program A SET of instructions that controls the operation of a computer.

cone The surface swept out by a line that is rotated about an axis while keeping one point (the vertex) fixed.

conic The curved shapes—ellipse, parabola, and hyperbola—obtained by the intersection of a plane with a cone. Also known as a conic section.

conic section See CONIC.

continuum hypothesis The principle of SET THEORY stating that every infinite subset of REAL NUMBERS is either countable or has the cardinality of the continuum.

coordinates The numbers indicating the location of a point on a plane or in a higher-dimensional space.

cosine For an acute angle in a right triangle, the ratio of the adjacent side to the hypotenuse.

countable An infinite SET is countable if it can be put into a one-to-one correspondence with the set of NATURAL NUMBERS.

coxcomb diagram See POLAR AREA DIAGRAM.

cryptography The study of coding and decoding secret messages.

cube (1) A regular solid having six congruent faces, each of which is a square. (2) To multiply a quantity times itself three times; raise to the third power.

cubic (1) A polynomial of degree 3. (2) An equation or curve (graph) corresponding to a cubic polynomial.

degree (1) A unit of angle measure equal to 1/360 of a circle. (2) The number of edges that meet at a vertex in a polygon or polyhedron. (3) The sum of the exponents of all the variables occurring in a term of a polynomial or algebraic expression.

degree of a polynomial or equation The highest exponent occurring in any of its terms.

derivative A function formed as the limit of a ratio of differences of the values of another function. One of two fundamental ideas of calculus that indicates the rate at which a quantity is changing.

diagonal In a square or a rectangle, the line joining two opposite corners.

diagonal argument A proof technique popularized by Georg Cantor in which an infinite array of numbers is manipulated by traversing the array along a diagonal.

diameter (1) The distance across a circle. (2) A line segment of this length passing through the center of a circle joining two points on opposite sides of the circle.

Difference Engine A hand-cranked, mechanical computer designed and built in the 1820s by Charles Babbage that used the method of finite differences to calculate and print mathematical, navigational, and astronomical tables with six-digits of accuracy.

differential equation An equation involving derivatives.

differential geometry The branch of mathematics dealing with the study of curved surfaces.

differentiation The process of determining the DERIVATIVE of a function.

divisible A number is divisible by another if the resulting quotient has no remainder.

elasticity The property of a substance that determines it ability to bend, stretch, and vibrate.

ellipse The intersection of a cone with a plane that meets the cone in a closed curve. Equivalently, the SET of points whose distances from two fixed points, called the foci of the ellipse, have a constant sum.

elliptic function A doubly periodic function that is the inverse of an elliptic integral.

elliptic integral An integral related to the length of an arc of an ELLIPSE.

encryption The process of translating a message into a secret code.

entire function A function whose DERIVATIVE is defined for all complex numbers.

equation A mathematical sentence stating that two algebraic expressions or numerical quantities have the same value.

equipollent Having the same cardinality.

Euler-Poincaré characteristic A topological constant of a surface determined by adding and subtracting the number of geometrical shapes of each dimension that make up the surface.

even number An integer that can be written as two times another integer.

exponent A number indicating how many repeated factors of the quantity occur. Also known as power.

factor An INTEGER that divides a given integer without leaving a remainder.

Fermat prime A PRIME NUMBER of the form $2^{2^n} + 1$ for some positive integer n.

Fermat's last theorem A principle in NUMBER THEORY conjectured by Pierre de Fermat stating that there are no positive integers x, y, and z that satisfy the equation $x^n + y^n = z^n$ for any integer $n > 3$.

finite difference method A numerical procedure used to evaluate a POLYNOMIAL of degree n by combining related values in a table having n columns. Supplied with the initial value in each column and the same constant value for all entries in the last column, each subsequent value in the first $n - 1$ columns is calculated as the sum of the two entries directly above it and to its right.

Fourier series An infinite series whose terms are of the form $a_n \sin(nx)$ and $b_n \cos(nx)$.

fraction See RATIONAL NUMBER.

fuchsian function See AUTOMORPHIC FUNCTION.

functional analysis The branch of mathematics dealing with the investigation of properties of sets of functions.

fundamental theorem of algebra The principle that every polynomial equation of one variable with real coefficients can be written as a product of factors of the first or second degree with real coefficients.

fundamental theorem of arithmetic The principle that each positive integer can be written as a product of PRIME NUMBERS in only one way.

Galois theory The branch of abstract algebra concerned with the study of sequences of groups that are related to the solutions of polynomial equations.

Gaussian curvature A numerical value indicating the manner in which a surface is curved.

Gaussian integer A complex number that can be written as the sum of an integer and the square root of a negative integer.

Gauss's law One of the four Maxwell equations that present a unified electromagnetic theory, this principle discovered by Carl Friedrich Gauss states that the electric flux through any closed surface is proportional to the net electric charge enclosed by the surface.

general binomial theorem The statement that the sum of two quantities raised to any real or complex power can be written as a finite or infinite sum of terms using the generalized binomial coefficients according to the formula

$$(a+b)^n = a^n + \binom{n}{1}a^{n-1}b + \binom{n}{2}a^{n-2}b^2 + \binom{n}{3}a^{n-3}b^3 + \cdots .$$

generalized binomial coefficient An integer or fractional value given by the computation $\binom{n}{k} = \dfrac{n(n-1)(n-2)\ldots(n-k+1)}{k\,(k-1)(k-2)\cdots 1}$ where k is an integer and n is an integer, fractional, real, or complex value. When n is a positive integer this computation agrees with the binomial coefficient.

genus An invariant numerical quantity of a surface or function.

geodesy The scientific study of land measurement and mapmaking.

geometric series An infinite sum of the form

$$a + ar + ar^2 + ar^3 + \ldots .$$

geometry The mathematical study of shapes, forms, their transformations, and the spaces that contain them.

graph theory The branch of mathematics in which relationships between objects are represented by a collection of vertices and edges.

gravitation The attractive force that pulls objects toward one other.

group theory The branch of abstract algebra dealing with the structure, properties, and interaction of groups—SETS of objects that can be combined with an operation that satisfies four basic conditions.

hydrostatics The study of the properties of fluids.

hyperbola The intersection of a cone with a plane that intersects both nappes of the cone. Equivalently, the SET of points whose distances from two fixed points, called the foci of the hyperbola, have a constant difference.

integer A whole number such as –4, –1, 0, 2, or 5.

integral A function formed as the limit of a sum of terms defined by another function. One of two fundamental ideas of calculus that can be used to find the area under a curve.

integration The process of determining the integral of a function.

intersect To cross or meet.

irrational number A REAL NUMBER such as $\sqrt{2}$ or π that cannot be expressed as a ratio of two integers.

least squares A numerical method to produce the equation of the line or curve that passes as close as possible to the points in a given set of data.

line diagram A graphical presentation of statistical information in which the length of each line segment in the diagram is proportional to the value of the corresponding datum.

mechanics The branch of physics dealing with the laws of motion.

natural number One of the positive numbers 1, 2, 3, 4, 5, . . .

negative number Any number whose value is less than zero.

number theory The mathematical study of the properties of positive integers.

odd number An integer that is not an even number, that cannot be written as two times another integer.

one-to-one correspondence A systematic pairing of the elements of two SETS in which each element of the first set is paired with one element of the second set and vice versa.

optics The branch of the physical sciences dealing with properties of light and vision.

orbit The path of one heavenly body around another such as the Moon's orbit around Earth or Earth's orbit around the Sun.

parabola The intersection of a cone with a plane that intersects one nappe of the cone but not in a closed curve. Equivalently, the set of points equidistant from a fixed point, called the focus of the parabola, and from a fixed line called the directrix of the parabola.

parallel postulate The axiom stated by Euclid of Alexandria that for a given point and line, there is only one line that can be drawn through the point that does not eventually meet the given line.

partial differential equation An equation involving the derivatives of a function of several variables.

perfect square See SQUARE NUMBER.

perimeter The sum of the lengths of the sides of a polygon.

periodic function A function whose values repeat on a regular basis. A function $f(x)$ is a periodic function if there is some constant k called its period so that $f(x + k) = f(x)$ for all values of x.

philology The study of languages.

pi (π) The ratio of the circumference a circle to its diameter, approximately 3.14159.

Poincaré conjecture A claim made by Henri Poincaré stating that any n-dimensional surface sharing certain properties with the n-sphere was topologically equivalent to the n-sphere.

polar area diagram A graphical presentation of statistical information invented by Florence Nightingale in which the area of each wedge-shaped region of a diagram is proportional to the value of the corresponding datum. Also known as a coxcomb diagram.

polygon A planar region bounded by segments. The segments bounding the polygon are its sides and their endpoints are its vertices.

polyhedron A solid bounded by polygons. The polygons bounding the polyhedron are its faces; the sides of the polygons are its edges; the vertices of the polygons and its vertices.

polynomial An algebraic expression that is the sum of the products of numbers and variables.

positive number Any number whose value is less than zero.

postulate See AXIOM.

power See EXPONENT.

power series A representation of a function as an infinite sum of terms in which each term includes a power of the variable.

power set The set of all subsets of a given SET.

prime number An integer greater than 1 that cannot be divided by any positive integer other than itself and 1. The first few prime numbers are 2, 3, 5, 7, 11, 13, 17, . . .

probability theory The branch of mathematics concerned with the systematic determination of numerical values to indicate the likelihood of the occurrence of events.

proof The logical reasoning that establishes the validity of a THEOREM from definitions, AXIOMS, and previously proved results.

proper divisor For any positive integer, those smaller positive numbers that divide it.

proper subset A SET containing some but not all of the elements of a given set.

proportion An equality of ratios of the form $a/b = c/d$.

Pythagorean Theorem The rule about right triangles proven by Pythagoras of Samos that states: If a, b, and c are the lengths of the three sides of a triangle, then the triangle is a right triangle if and only if $a^2 + b^2 = c^2$.

quadratic equation An equation of the form $ax^2 + bx + c = 0$.

quadratic formula The formula that gives the 0, 1, or 2 solutions to a quadratic equation as $x = \dfrac{-b \pm \sqrt{b^2 - 4ac}}{2a}$.

quadratic reciprocity A property in number theory that determines whether a pair of odd PRIME NUMBERS can be repeatedly added to produce infinitely many perfect squares.

quintic equation A polynomial equation with degree five of the form $a_5x^5 + a_4x^4 + a_3x^3 + a_2x^2 + a_1x + a_0 = 0$.

quintic formula A nonexistent formula that would solve every quintic equation in finitely many steps using only the operations of addition, subtraction, multiplication, division, and the taking of roots.

radius (1) The distance from the center of a circle to any point on its circumference. (2) A line segment of this length with one endpoint at the center of a circle and the other endpoint located on its circumference.

radius of convergence Half the width of the interval of values for which a POWER SERIES sums to a finite total.

ratio The fraction obtained by dividing one number by another.

rational number A number that can be expressed as a ratio of two integers. Also known as a fraction.

real number One of the set of numbers that includes zero, the positive and negative integers, the rationals, and the irrationals.

regular polygon A two-dimensional polygon such as an equilateral triangle or a square in which all sides are congruent to one another and all angles are congruent to one another.

right angle An angle with measure 90°.

right triangle A triangle with one right angle.

root (1) A solution to an equation. (2) A number that when repeatedly multiplied produces a given numerical value.

ruler-and-compass construction A plane geometrical diagram that can be created with the use of a ruler or straight edge to draw line segments and a compass to replicate distances and draw circular arcs.

sequence An infinitely long list of values that follow a pattern.

series An infinite sum of numbers or terms.

set A well-defined collection of objects.

set theory The branch of mathematics dealing with relationships between SETS.

simultaneous equations   Two or more equations relating the same variables that are to be solved at the same time. Also known as a system of equations.

sine   For an acute angle in a right triangle, the ratio of the opposite side to the hypotenuse.

solvable by radicals   A polynomial equation is solvable by radicals if its solution can be determined in finitely many steps using only the operations of addition, subtraction, multiplication, division, and the taking of roots.

Sophie Germain prime number   A prime number p for which $2p + 1$ is also prime.

special theory of relativity   A theory in physics developed by Albert Einstein to explain the properties of space, matter, and time.

sphere   The set of all points in three-dimensional space at a given distance, called the radius, from a fixed point, called the center.

spiral   A planar curve traced out by a point rotating about a fixed point while simultaneously moving away from the fixed point.

square   (1) A four-sided polygon with all sides congruent to one another and all angles congruent to one another. (2) To multiply a quantity times itself; raise to the second power.

square number   A positive integer that can be written as n^2 for some integer n. Also known as a perfect square.

statistics   The branch of mathematics dealing with the collecting, tabulating, and summarizing numerical information obtained from observational or experimental studies and drawing conclusions about the population from which the data was selected.

system of equations   See SIMULTANEOUS EQUATIONS.

tangent   For an acute angle in a right triangle, the ratio of the opposite side to the adjacent side.

theorem   A mathematical property or rule.

three-body problem   A classical situation in celestial mechanics dealing with the positions and motions of three heavenly bodies, such as the Sun, Earth, and the Moon, resulting from their mutual gravitational attraction.

transcendental number   A real number that is not the root of an algebraic equation.

transfinite number A number that gives the cardinality of an infinite SET.

triangle A polygon with three vertices and three edges.

trichotomy of cardinals The principle of SET THEORY stating that for any two sets A and B, the cardinality of set A must be greater than, less than, or equal to the cardinality of set B.

trigonometric functions The functions $\sin(x)$, $\cos(x)$, and $\tan(x)$ that form the basis of the study of trigonometry.

trigonometry The study of right triangles and the relationships among the measurements of their angles and sides.

uncountable An infinite set is uncountable if it cannot be put into a one-to-one correspondence with the set of natural numbers.

unit interval The set of all real numbers between 0 and 1, written as [0, 1] or as $\{|0 \leq x \leq 1\}$.

unit square The set of all points in the x-y plane whose coordinates lie between 0 and 1, written as $\{(x, y)|0 \leq x, y \leq 1\}$.

variable A letter used to represent an unknown or unspecified quantity.

vertex The endpoint of a segment in a geometric figure.

well-ordering principle The principle from SET THEORY that every nonempty SET has a smallest element.

FURTHER READING

Books

Ashurst, F. Gareth. *Founders of Modern Mathematics*. London: Muller, 1982. Biographies of selected prominent mathematicians.

Ball, W. W. Rouse. *A Short Account of the History of Mathematics*. New York: Dover, 1960. Reprint of 1908 edition of the classic history of mathematics covering the period from 600 B.C.E. to 1900.

Bell, Eric T. *Men of Mathematics*. New York: Simon & Schuster, 1965. The classic history of European mathematics from 1600 to 1900 organized around the lives of 30 influential mathematicians.

Boyer, Carl, and Uta Merzbach. *A History of Mathematics*. 2nd ed. New York: Wiley, 1991. A history of mathematics organized by eras from prehistoric times through the mid-20th century, for more advanced audiences.

Burton, David M. *The History of Mathematics. An Introduction*. 2nd ed. Dubuque, Iowa: Brown, 1988. Very readable college textbook on the history of mathematics through the end of the 19th century with biographical sketches throughout.

Dunham, William. *Journey through Genius. The Great Theorems of Mathematics*. New York: Wiley, 1990. Presentation of 12 mathematical ideas focusing on their historical development, the lives of the mathematicians involved, and the proofs of these theorems.

———. *The Mathematical Universe. An Alphabetical Journey through the Great Proofs, Problems, and Personalities*. New York: Wiley, 1994. Presentation of 26 topics in mathematics focusing on their historical development, the lives of the mathematicians involved, and the reasons these theorems are valid.

Eves, Howard. *Great Moments in Mathematics (Before 1650)*. Washington, D.C.: Mathematical Association of America, 1983. Presentation of 20 major mathematical discoveries that occurred before 1650 and the mathematicians involved.

——. *Great Moments in Mathematics (After 1650)*. Washington, D.C.: Mathematical Association of America, 1981. Presentation of major mathematical discoveries that occurred after 1650 and the mathematicians involved.

——. *An Introduction to the History of Mathematics*. 3rd ed. New York: Holt, Rinehart and Winston, 1969. An undergraduate textbook covering the history of mathematical topics through elementary calculus, accessible to high school students.

Gillispie, Charles C., ed. *Dictionary of Scientific Biography*. 18 vols. New York: Scribner, 1970–1980. Multivolume encyclopedia presenting biographies of thousands of mathematicians and scientists, for adult audiences.

Grinstein, Louise S., and Paul J. Campbell, eds. *Women of Mathematics: A Biobibliographic Sourcebook*. New York: Greenwood, 1987. Biographical profiles of 43 women each with an extensive list of references.

Henderson, Harry. *Modern Mathematicians*. New York: Facts On File, 1996. Profiles of 13 mathematicians from the 19th and 20th centuries.

James, Ioan M. *Remarkable Mathematicians: From Euler to von Neumann*. Cambridge: Cambridge University Press, 2002. Profiles of 60 mathematicians from the 18th, 19th and 20th centuries.

Katz, Victor J. *A History of Mathematics: An Introduction*, 2nd ed. Reading, Mass.: Addison Wesley Longmann, 1998. College textbook, explains accessible portions of mathematical works and provides brief biographical sketches.

Morrow, Charlene, and Teri Perl, eds. *Notable Women in Mathematics: A Biographical Dictionary*. Westport, Conn.: Greenwood, 1998. Short biographies of 59 women mathematicians, including many 20th century figures.

Muir, Jane. *Of Men and Numbers, the Story of the Great Mathematicians.* New York: Dover, 1996. Short profiles of mathematicians.

Newman, James R., ed. *The World of Mathematics.* 4 vols. New York: Simon & Schuster, 1956. Collection of essays about topics in mathematics including the history of mathematics.

Osen, Lynn M. *Women in Mathematics.* Cambridge, Mass.: MIT Press, 1974. Biographies of 8 women mathematicians through the early 20th century.

Perl, Teri. *Math Equals: Biographies of Women Mathematicians + Related Activities.* Menlo Park, Calif.: Addison Wesley, 1978. Biographies of 10 women mathematicians through the early 20th century, each accompanied by exercises related to their mathematical work.

Reimer, Luetta, and Wilbert Reimer. *Mathematicians Are People, Too, Stories from the Lives of Great Mathematicians.* Parsippany, N.J.: Seymour, 1990. Collection of stories about 15 mathematicians with historical facts and fictionalized dialogue, intended for elementary school students.

———. *Mathematicians Are People, Too, Stories from the Lives of Great Mathematicians.* vol. 2. Parsippany, N.J.: Seymour, 1995. Collection of stories about 15 more mathematicians with historical facts and fictionalized dialogue, intended for elementary school students.

Reimer, Wilbert, and Luetta Reimer. *Historical Connections in Mathematics.* 2 vols. Fresno, Calif.: AIMS Educational Foundation, 1992–93. Each volume includes brief portraits of 10 mathematicians with worksheets related to their mathematical discoveries, for elementary school students.

Stillwell, John. *Mathematics and Its History.* New York: Springer-Verlag, 1989. Undergraduate textbook organized around 20 topics each developed in their historical context.

Struik, D. J. *A Source Book in Mathematics 1200–1800.* Cambridge, Mass.: Harvard University Press, 1969. Excerpts with commentary from 75 of the influential mathematical manuscripts of the period.

Struik, Dirk J. *A Concise History of Mathematics.* 4th revised ed. New York: Dover, 1987. Brief history of mathematics through the first half of the 20th century with extensive multilingual biographical references.

Tabak, John. *The History of Mathematics*. 5 vols. New York: Facts On File, 2004. Important events and prominent individuals in the development of the major branches of mathematics, for grades 6 and up.

Tanton, James. *Encyclopedia of Mathematics*. New York: Facts On File, 2005. Articles and essays about events, ideas, and people in mathematics, for grades 9 and up.

Turnbull, Herbert W. *The Great Mathematicians*. New York: New York University Press, 1961. Profiles of six mathematicians with more detail than most sources.

Young, Robin V., ed. *Notable Mathematicians from Ancient Times to the Present*. Detroit, Mich.: Gale, 1998. Short profiles of mathematicians.

Internet Resources

Agnes Scott College. "Biographies of Women Mathematicians," Available online. URL: http://www.agnesscott.edu/lriddle/women/women.htm. Accessed on March 4, 2005. Biographies of more than 100 women mathematicians prepared by students at Agnes Scott College, Decatur, GA.

Bellevue Community College. "Mathographies," Available online. URL: http://scidiv.bcc.ctc.edu/Math/MathFolks.html. Accessed on March 4, 2005. Brief biographies of 25 mathematicians prepared by faculty members at Bellevue Community College, Bellevue, Wash.

Drexel University. "Math Forum," Available online. URL: http://www.mathforum.org/. Accessed on March 3, 2005. Site for mathematics and mathematics education, includes "Problem of the Week," "Ask Dr. Math," and *Historia-Matematica* discussion group, by School of Education at Drexel University, Philadelphia, Pa.

Miller, Jeff. "Images of Mathematicians on Postage Stamps," Available online. URL: http://jeff560.tripod.com/. Accessed on March 6, 2005. Images of hundreds of mathematicians and mathematical topics on international stamps with link to Web ring of mathematical stamp collecting, by high school math teacher Jeff Miller.

National Association of Mathematics. "Mathematicians of the African Diaspora," Available online. URL: http://www.math.buffalo.edu/mad/. Accessed on March 1, 2005. Includes profiles of 250 black mathematicians and historical information about mathematics in ancient Africa.

Rice University. "Galileo Project Catalog of the Scientific Community in the 16th and 17th Centuries," Avaliable online. URL: http://galileo.rice.edu/lib/catalog.html. Accessed on July 5, 2005. Biographical outlines of 600 members mathematicians and scientists of the period compiled by the late Professor Richard Westfall of Indiana University.

Scienceworld. "Eric Weisstein's World of Scientific Biography," Available online. URL: http://scienceworld.wolfram.com/biography/. Accessed on February 12, 2005. Brief profiles of more than 250 mathematicians and hundreds of other scientists. Link to related site Mathworld, an interactive mathematics encyclopedia providing access to numerous articles about historical topics and extensive discussions of mathematical terms and ideas, by Eric Weisstein of Wolfram Research.

Simon Fraser University. "History of Mathematics," Available online. URL: http//www.math.sfu.ca/histmath. Accessed on January 19, 2005. A collection of short profiles of a dozen mathematicians, from Simon Fraser University, Burnaby, British Columbia, Canada.

University of Saint Andrews. "MacTutor History of Mathematics Archive," Available online. URL: http://www-groups.dcs.st-andrews.ac.uk/~history. Accessed on March 5, 2005. Searchable, online index of mathematical history and biographies of more than 2,000 mathematicians, from the University of Saint Andrews, Scotland.

University of Tennessee. "Math Archives," Available online. URL: http://archives.math.utk.edu/topics/history.html. Accessed on December 10, 2004. Ideas for teaching mathematics and links to Web sites about the history of mathematics and other mathematical topics, by the University of Tennessee, Knoxville.

The Wikimedia Foundation. "Wikipedia: The Free Encyclopedia: Mathematics," Available online. URL: http://en.wikipedia.org/wiki/Mathematics. Accessed on August 22, 2005. Online biographies with many links to in-depth explanations of related mathematical topics.

ASSOCIATIONS

Association for Women in Mathematics (www.awm-math.org) 4114 Computer and Space Sciences Building, University of Maryland, College Park, Md. 20742-2461. Telephone: 301-405-7892. Professional society for female mathematics professors, Web site includes link to biographies of women in mathematics.

Mathematical Association of America (www.maa.org) 1529 18th Street NW, Washington, D.C. 20036. Telephone: 202-387-5200. Professional society for college mathematics professors, Web site includes link to the association's History of Mathematics Special Interest Group (HOM SIGMAA).

National Association of Mathematicians (www.math.buffalo.edu/mad/NAM/) Department of Mathematics, 244 Mathematics Building, University at Buffalo, Buffalo, N.Y. 14260-2900. Professional society focusing on needs of underrepresented American minorities in mathematics.

National Council of Teachers of Mathematics (www.nctm.org) 1906 Association Drive, Reston, Va. 20191-1502. Telephone: 703-620-9840. Professional society for mathematics teachers.

Index